Girlfriend REVIVAL

Praise for Revival

Girlfriend Revival has a powerful and thought provoking message for anyone looking for purpose and destiny. Through her "ups and downs", "in's and out's", "highs and low's", Danielle's story will have you sitting on the edge of your seat. Her real and raw approach to story is both refreshing and authentic. Revival means to make new again, and that is what her story is about. If you need hope, help, or simply just a fresh new beginning this book is for you.

~ **Tammy Hotsenpiller**
Women of Influence Founder and President
Author of *3 Skips and a Jump to Becoming a Woman of Influence*

It's easy to find a book of devotions geared toward women, but it's not easy to find a book that is as honest, relatable, gripping and meaningful as Danielle Augustin's *Girlfriend Revival*. Early into her book, Danielle begins to feel like your girlfriend: someone you know intimately, and someone with whom you could share your own hopes and dreams. The best gift of *Girlfriend Revival*, though, is hope. Through abandonment, illness, broken relationships – Danielle retains a flexible and enduring faith that will awaken your own *Girlfriend Revival*.

~ **The Rev. Angela Denker**
Lutheran Pastor and Faith Writer/Blogger
Teaching Pastor, Easter Lutheran Church: Minneapolis, MN
Author of *Red State Christians* and blogger at
A Good Christian Woman ... Not that One

Sometimes gritty and raw, sometimes warm and uplifting, *Girlfriend Revival* is a beautifully written book that invites the reader to reimagine and redefine what might otherwise be considered failure, pain, or problems. By sharing her own stories of loss, fear, triumph and defeat, Danielle helps the reader to see that given the right perspective, these experiences are all opportunities for reinvention. What may seem or feel or look like a failure to the naked eye can actually be viewed as an opportunity for growth, change and enrichment. *Girlfriend Revival* helps readers to discard their secular lens and look at their personal challenges through the eyes of God in a way that empowers them to transform their experiences and their lives.

~ **Dr. Dani Wilson**
Dean, Library/Learning Resources, Instructional Support Programs and Services
Fullerton College

Danielle pours her heart out with courage, strength and empowerment, inspiring the reader to rise above hardships, move forward toward joy, and tune into God for utmost fulfillment. This book is touching and a must read for women wanting their best life.

~ **Kim Somers Egelsee**
Confidence Expert, Business and Life Coach
#1 Bestselling Author of *Getting Your Life to a 10 Plus*
Award Winning TEDx Speaker

Girlfriend REVIVAL

Awaken YOUR FAITH
STEP INTO YOUR DIVINE Destiny

DANIELLE AUGUSTIN

Copyright © 2018 Danielle Augustin

All rights reserved.
No portion of this book may be reproduced mechanically, electronically, or by any other means, including photocopying, without written permission of the publisher. It is illegal to copy this book, post it to a website, or distribute it by any other means without permission from the publisher.

Get Branded Press
Huntington Beach, CA 92648
www.GetBrandedPress.com

Limits of Liability and Disclaimer of Warranty.
The author and publisher shall not be liable for your misuse of this material. This book is strictly for informational and educational purposes.

Warning – Disclaimer.
The purpose of this book is to educate and entertain. The author and/or publisher do not guarantee that anyone following these techniques, suggestions, tips, ideas, or strategies will become successful. The author and/or publisher shall have neither liability nor responsibility to anyone with respect to any loss or damage caused, or alleged to be caused, directly or indirectly by the information contained in this book.

ISBN 978-1-944807-04-7 paperback
ISBN 978-1-944807-05-4 ebook
ISBN 978-1-944807-06-1 audiobook
Library of Congress Cataloging-in-Publishing Data is available upon request.

Printed in the United States of America
First Printing, 2018

Edited by Taylor Augustin www.GetBrandedPress.com
Cover & Interior Design by Kate Korniienko-Heidtman
Cover Photography by Allan Helmick

Dedication

*For my mother, Gale, who taught me to cherish
every moment and be grateful
for the simple things.*

Gratitude

I'm so grateful for all of the love and support that my friends and family have shown me throughout the creation of this project. I could not have done it without all of you.

To my husband, best friend and biggest supporter – thank you Craig for ALWAYS believing in me, no matter how many crazy ideas I come up with. I couldn't imagine riding this rollercoaster of life with anyone else. You are the most selfless human being I know and I'm so inspired by the example you live out each and every day. The hundreds of prayer walks together at the park, are moments in time I'll cherish forever and have given me such peace and inspiration. I like the rollercoaster. I love you!

To my children, Taylor, TJ, Luke and Gracie, you are precious gifts in my life and I'm so honored to be your mom. When I look at you, I see God's miracles. Your love and support mean the world to me. I love you deeply.

A very special thank you to my daughter Taylor, for all the times you stayed up late, reviewing and editing endless drafts of this book. Your suggestions and insight have been invaluable. You have grown to be an amazing woman and a very talented writer. Your future is bright and I'm so proud of you.

To Susie Augustin at Get Branded Press, I'm so grateful for your love, support, advice and inspiration. Thank you for believing in me. I couldn't have done this without you. You are a book publishing and marketing ROCKSTAR! And special thanks to Kate Korniienko-Heidtman for creating the book layout and beautiful cover design.

To my marketing guru, Rasheed Lewis at Epiphany Marketing, you are the best. Thank you for your creative mind, diligence and vision for this project among many others. You've brought my dream to life and I'm so grateful.

To my friends Dr. Dani Wilson and Elizabeth Curtis, thank you for the time you took to give me the crucial feedback necessary to bring this book to publication.

To my friend Tammy Hotsenpiller, thank you for being such an inspiration to me. Your encouragement and support have been invaluable.

Thank you to Kim Somers Egelsee for your brilliant ideas and for supporting me through this project.

To my Lord and Savior Jesus Christ, thank you for breathing life into me, walking beside me and inspiring me to chase after the dreams you have placed on my heart. I can't wait for the next adventure. I'm ready to dive in, trusting you will equip me with everything I need. I pray your Spirit anoints my life and that you continue providing me discernment, so that I can tell the world about your extraordinary love and promise of eternity in heaven with you.

Contents

Introduction ... 12

Part One DERAILED

1. Heavenly Equipped ... 18
2. Six Months ... 20
3. Take Off Your Wig & Live ... 22
4. Moments that Remain ... 24
5. No Words Required ... 26
6. An Eternal Bond ... 27
7. From Runaway to Revival ... 30
8. Starting Over ... 33
9. A New Forever Family ... 35

Part Two POWER

10. Slow Down and Listen ... 40
11. Community Counts ... 42
12. God's Got This ... 43
13. Be Present ... 46
14. The Waiting Room ... 47
15. Even if the Mountain Doesn't Move ... 49
16. The Day That Changed Me ... 51
17. Ignore and Believe ... 53
18. Life is Precious ... 55
19. I'm Here ... 56
20. Hurry Up & Slow Down ... 58
21. An Appointment with Destiny ... 60
22. Picture Perfect ... 62
23. Time with God ... 63
24. A Beautiful Song ... 65
25. #Incredobill ... 67
26. Slave No More ... 69
27. Unshakable Identity ... 70

Part Three LOVE

28. Love Prevails — 76
29. Brutally Honest — 78
30. We're Going to Be Best Friends — 80
31. The Swing Set — 82
32. The Letter — 84
33. Everyday Moments — 86
34. The Crying Bench — 87
35. A Selfless Love — 89
36. Lessons of Love in a Grocery Store — 90
37. Get Dirty — 93
38. Progress Not Perfection — 95
39. Make Time — 96

Part Four COMMISSIONED

40. Right on Time — 102
41. The Granola Bar — 104
42. Take Care of You — 106
43. Enjoy the Ride — 108
44. Walking in Power — 110
45. It's Worth It — 112
46. Thankful for All of It — 114
47. Surrounded by Inspiration — 116
48. A Walk with God — 118
49. Whispers of Truth — 120
50. Too Much & Not Enough — 123
51. Seeking a Breakthrough — 125
52. Revival is Coming — 127

Final Thoughts — 129
About the Author — 131
Scriptural References — 134
Notes, Prayers and Dreams FOR REVIVAL — 136

Introduction

The first time I ran away from home, I was five years old. I was a bit of a dramatic child – maybe even a little stubborn. When I didn't get what I wanted at the moment it was demanded, I often used the threat of running away as a bargaining chip and it usually worked. On this particular day, however, I decided I would follow through on my threat. To my surprise, my mother supported this life-changing decision and even helped me pack up my red wagon for the journey. Filled primarily with dolls and toys, a few blankets and not nearly enough clothes, I was ready to go. I was quite confident heading out the door. Wagon in tow and on my way to a new life, my mother reminded me I may need some food to take with me. Without skipping a beat, I ran back into the house to fill my wagon with a bag full of canned food items (with no can opener of course).

As I set out on my new solo adventure, my mother gave me a hug and kiss at the end of the driveway, then wished me luck. Cue climactic music and you've got an Oscar-award winning movie scene as I waved goodbye in melodramatic fashion. Pulling my wagon down the street gave me such a sense of accomplishment and eager anticipation of the new life I was going to make. I would eat all the junk food I could imagine and stay up at night until I felt like going to bed. I would make my own decisions with no one to answer to. I was free! Yet with each step I took and house I passed along the way, I began to ponder what my actual plan was. It didn't take long before I realized, I didn't have a plan. Panic set in. It was at that moment, I cautiously looked over my shoulder to see my mother quietly following behind me, only a few houses away. It was her presence that gave me the confidence to keep walking. I ended up walking a perfect square around my neighborhood, and wouldn't you know it, I ended up back at my house with my mother right behind me.

My runaway expedition may have been short lived, but in the

end, the experience taught me more than I knew at the time. I eventually grasped the significance of this event and how God works in our lives. No matter how far off of God's path we may go, He will always be there to love, protect and guide us back to life. His plan is always better than ours and transpires in His time. He allows us to go through challenging times so that we are prepared and strengthened for the amazing journey He has for our lives.

This book contains some of my life's stories and lessons I've learned and want to share with you. I don't profess to have all of the answers to life's difficulties and I'm definitely still a work in progress. However, I've learned through some of the most painful experiences and incredible blessings to find beautiful meaning in the life I've been given. Girlfriend Revival will inspire you to embrace your story, live a life of love and awaken your faith. Only then, will you be able to step into the destiny God has prepared you for.

This book is grounded in my faith in God, the God of the Bible, and His son Jesus Christ. It is my hope that you will find time each day to read, journal, pray and speak with God. I invite you to use this book as a tool toward a path of knowing God's will for you, viewing the world through His eyes of perfect love. Each story is numbered, but not necessarily meant for daily affirmations. The intent of the stories coupled with scripture and prayer, is to provide you with enough to ponder, meditate and pray over. Some of the stories are funny and heartwarming, while others are tragic and painful. Each of them were experienced by me on my crooked and beautiful path to discovering God's love, His call upon my life and His abundance of blessings. I've also included space in the back of the book for you to journal your deepest thoughts, prayers and dreams.

Regardless of your faith, please know these lessons are for you. I pray you will come to know the God I love – a God who desperately loves you and wants to spend eternity with you. Perhaps my story will shed some light on Him and how

He relates to and deeply cares for His children. Believing in God doesn't guarantee you won't experience difficulties and hardship. Far from it. But, I can tell you He is always present with you through every blessing, tragedy and victory. He is a God who keeps His promises and He will never let you go.

We all have a story to share. You have an amazing story! You are not an accident. God created you in His image, and you are His precious child. If you knew the plans He has for you now, it would blow your mind. It doesn't matter your age; you have an incredible God-ordained life to live. The God of the universe breathed life into you, loves you and created you for a purpose. I pray you will grow closer to Him by hearing Him whisper His deepest thoughts to you through your story and life experiences, so you can fulfill all He's called you to be.

The word revival means an awakening, a renewal, coming back to life or taking something old and creating something new. Throughout all of our lives, there will be instances where we need revival. Revival from pain, fear, doubt and uncertainty. Do you need revival in your life? Revival in your faith? Revival in your relationships? Revival in your attitude? When you embrace your story, move beyond fear and live a life of faith, you will experience revival leading to your destiny.

Living a life of revival isn't about doing, it's about being. We don't need to check off a list of accomplishments to earn God's favor, love and grace. He gives these to us freely! We are called to live a life reflecting the love of Jesus. But, this process doesn't happen overnight. Instead, sanctification is something that occurs over a lifetime – a lifetime of learning, falling down and getting back up again, as we are transformed into the image of Jesus. That's great news! So, when you ponder the question we all do at some point in our lives, "What is God's will for my life?" – the answer is simple. Just love! Once you choose to live a life of love, this spirit of love will spread like a wildfire, unable to be contained. Let's go on a journey together, down a path filled with lessons that will change your life and set you in the direction into the loving arms of God.

Do you see what this means—all these pioneers who blazed the way, all these veterans cheering us on? It means we'd better get on with it. Strip down, start running—and never quit! No extra spiritual fat, no parasitic sins. Keep your eyes on Jesus, who both began and finished this race we're in. Study how he did it. Because he never lost sight of where He was headed—that exhilarating finish in and with God—he could put up with anything along the way: Cross, shame, whatever. And now he's there, in the place of honor, right alongside God. When you find yourselves flagging in your faith, go over that story again, item by item, that long litany of hostility he plowed through. That will shoot adrenaline into your souls!

– Hebrews 12:1-3

1
Heavenly Equipped

> *Do you not know? Have you not heard? The LORD is the everlasting God, the Creator of the ends of the earth. He will not grow tired or weary, and His understanding no one can fathom. He gives strength to the weary and increases the power of the weak. Even youths grow tired and weary, and young men stumble and fall; but those who hope in the LORD will renew their strength. They will soar on wings like eagles; they will run and not grow weary, they will walk and not be faint.*
>
> *– Isaiah 40:28-31*

I've always been a dreamer. From an early age, I knew God had something wild in store for me, but I couldn't put my finger on it. Growing up, I was willing to try just about any activity. Soccer, softball, dance, track ... you name it, I tried it. I was always up for a new adventure or challenge. I even took ice-skating lessons for a while, convinced I was going to be the next Olympian. I think my mother didn't have the courage to tell me I wasn't that good. I excelled in softball, played on a travel ball team and was an all-star.

During my teenage years, however, I made some pretty poor decisions that resulted in lost friendships and letting many people down. I was paralyzed by the disappointment I felt at every turn and became convinced there was nothing I could actually accomplish, or at least nothing amounting to much. Eventually, I started to define myself by my circumstances and the choices I had made. If I would have fallen in line with the way I viewed myself, I never would have graduated from high school, let alone gone onto college, become a wife and mother and built a thriving career. But, God had bigger plans. I pushed through what everyone else thought about me and even what

I thought about myself. I started believing I could do anything through Him. I learned God had amazing plans for me and a unique call upon my life.

The Bible is filled with stories of people who didn't have much according to earthly standards, however, they were able to accomplish more than they would have ever thought possible. David defeated Goliath with a slingshot and five smooth stones. Jesus fed 5,000+ people with five loaves of bread and two fish. Sarah gave birth to a son at an age well-beyond child bearing years. They all accomplished far beyond their circumstances.

When God puts a call on your life, He isn't limited by what you have. If you take a step of faith and give Him all you have, God will do the rest. So often, we get stuck in a mindset believing lies that we don't have the ability, capacity or gifts to complete what we know in our heart we were meant to do. If we aren't careful, we can talk ourselves out of living what we were called to do. Or perhaps, someone else has voiced their opinion that you don't have what it takes. If you are convinced you don't have the ability to complete what God has called you to do, you're right. But God will give you provision beyond your resume, beyond your skill set and beyond your own ability. He will supernaturally step in at the right time just when you need it. His dreams for your life exceed your own dreams. You can't even fathom what He has planned for you. Don't allow anyone to talk you out of pursuing your destiny, even if that someone is you. Don't limit what God has in store for your life, but instead, get in agreement with Him. He doesn't only see who you are today, He sees all you will become. If God's hand is on your life, leading and guiding you, there's nothing that can stop you!

Has God laid a promise on your heart where you know you were called to do something? Do you feel you're lacking in ability and that you can't accomplish what you know God is asking you to do? This feeling can be very frustrating, but trust me, you are in the perfect position to get in agreement with Him and accept all of the eternal and God-given provisions for your life to make His dreams for you come true. It's not about you, it's about God and what He can do through you. You need to take yourself out of the equation and set your eyes upon Him. When you make God and His mission the focus, you are untouchable and will fulfill dreams that exceed your capacity, your experience and your ability to impact the world. When will you realize your destiny waits for you? His love is like a flowing river filled with an abundance of provision ready to overtake you. I pray you will jump in and let His grace overwhelm you, trusting in Him to provide exactly what you need – even if all you have are a few fish, a little bit of bread or a handful of stones.

Today's Prayer:
Lord, thank you for equipping me with everything I need to fulfill the dreams you have laid upon my heart, even when I feel I don't have the skills or ability to accomplish what I know you've called me to do. Today, I will step out in faith, trusting in your perfect plan for my life and fully grasp you will give me provision to be all you created me to be.

2
Six Months

> *For God gave us a spirit not of fear but of power and love and self-control.*
>
> – 2 Timothy 1:7

When I was three years old, my mother was diagnosed with terminal lymphoma. Given six months to live at the age of 26, along with a terminal illness, she put things in perspective pretty quickly. To make matters worse, my father was unable to care for my mother and I due to severe struggles with substance abuse, and he soon abandoned both of us. You've probably heard the song, "Live Like You Were Dying." I was blessed to witness my mother live her life in that exact way. Sometimes, I try to imagine what her life must've been like. I'm sure she was terrified on the inside, but I never saw it. As a single mother, she continued to work full time and went back to school to earn a college degree. She coached my softball teams, volunteered at my school and advocated for other people battling life-threatening illnesses. She was a force to be reckoned with, living each day as though it was her last. Although I wouldn't realize it until many years later, she taught me to cherish every moment simply by watching the way she lived.

Jesus walked the earth, pushing into the lives of sinners, social outcasts and the forgotten. And He knew exactly where He was going – the cross. Understanding His grim future and faced with ridicule and the threat of being arrested at every turn, He chose to live a life of love, humility and compassion. His life is a stunning reflection of the life we are called to live. A life grounded in love.

If I were given this same news, would I change the way I live my life? Would I look at the world around me differently, grasping the beauty of the simple things I so often take for granted? I think I would. I wouldn't focus on the little things that bother me. The red light that makes me late to an appointment, the stain on the carpet, my child walking too slow or the meal that wasn't cooked to my liking. Perhaps I'd realize I was blessed to live another day, drive through the hills of my community with the windows down, spend time with my family and make a home-cooked meal with my girlfriends.

The reality of an uncertain future can be crippling, halting us in our tracks. The overwhelming urge to crawl into bed, pull the covers over our heads, and drown out the reality swirling around us can be paralyzing. Yet, we can learn from people like my mother who choose to truly live in the face of devastating odds. Odds screaming there is no hope. However, instead of relenting to the negative health report, accepting your child will never turn around or your marriage will never be what it used to be, fight through the persistent fear and pain. Live a beautiful life because you choose love every day. Imagine what you could accomplish in just six months.

In six months, plant a garden.
In six months, write a book.
In six months, take that trip you've dreamed of.
In six months, forgive those who have hurt you.
In six months, find something to be grateful for every day.
In six months, love until your last breath.

Today's Prayer:
When I'm facing circumstances that appear too much for me to bear, I will lean on you God, and allow your overflowing love to overtake me, bringing me peace that can't be found anywhere but in you.

3
Take Off Your Wig & Live

> *I know what it is to be in need, and I know what it is to have plenty. I have learned the secret of being content in any and every situation, whether well fed or hungry, whether living in plenty or in want. I can do all this through Him who gives me strength.*
>
> *– Philippians 4:12-13*

Every detail of my 11th birthday party was planned out for months. This epic slumber party was going to be a night to remember. The games were endless, along with the junk food, soda and cake. Perhaps planning the party had taken my eyes and heart off of my mother's terminal illness that had come out of remission with a fury and rocked our world. I'm not sure what prompted my mother to do what she did – maybe I was in such shock, I blocked it from my memory. But, at the end of one of the many games we played throughout the night, she proceeded to take off her wig, exposing her perfectly bald head and replaced it with a headband with two stars on springs shooting to the sky. This was followed by her running through the house being chased by all of my friends. They absolutely loved it and loved her. However, I wasn't loving it at all. In fact, I was absolutely mortified. I wasn't chasing her with the gaggle of girls; I was hiding in the corner shooting her a look that screamed, "PLEASE PUT YOUR WIG BACK ON, YOU'RE RUINING MY PARTY." She didn't – and I'm so glad.

My mother chose to truly live each day because she knew she didn't have much time on this earth. I don't remember all of my birthday parties growing up, but I'll never forget my 11th birthday. Faced with an uncertain future and through immense pain, I witnessed a beautiful moment that modeled how we are to embrace each day and truly live no matter what our circumstance.

> *"We are hard pressed on every side, but*
> *not crushed; perplexed, but not in despair;*
> *persecuted, but not abandoned; struck down,*
> *but not destroyed" (2 Corinthians 4:8-9).*

We can learn a lot by watching the courage of other people. It's infectious to see someone live a life of true joy in the face of suffering and pain. It's all about perspective. Some people look at life like a cup that is half-empty, while others look at it as half-full. But in reality, life is like an overflowing cup filled with God's grace, spilling out His love through you for the world to experience. When you are faced with life's unexpected raging river trying to sweep you away, fight the urge to sink into fear and instead cling to the promise you have in God. Keep your eyes fixed on Him instead of the reality swirling all around you. Dive into what He says about you in His Word. He is your anchor. He is your joy. Remember ...

Be genuine to who you really are, not who the world says you should be.

Live with joy in your heart.

Find beauty every day.

Give and be thankful.

Have fun.

Pray.

Love ... always.

Today's Prayer:
Lord, guide my ways and help me to push through any circumstance I'm faced with so I can truly embrace each day and be thankful in every situation. I will look for joy all around me and spread it contagiously so others around me see you in all I do.

4
Moments That Remain

> *And the peace of God, which transcends all understanding, will guard your hearts and your minds in Christ Jesus.*
>
> *– Philippians 4:7*

When my mother was nearing the end of her time on earth, it was extremely difficult for me to watch her suffer, helpless to provide any reprieve for her pain. I was a very confused 15-year-old teenager, unable to deal with the overwhelming emotions of fear and anger that had taken over me. My mother wanted to be home for her last days, but her pain became so severe, she required specialized care at the hospital. Perhaps having her at the hospital was God's way of protecting me from seeing her each day slipping further away from me, and closer to Jesus. Her pain was so relentless, she needed extensive medication which left her unaware of what was going on around her. Her body was covered with bruises from head to toe, which I found out later were tumors. Her speech was slurred and her hair was gone. The vivacious woman I knew her to be was slowly fading away. Her hospital room was always filled with friends and family saying their last goodbyes, but she was mostly unaware of what was going on and who was there. There were seemingly endless tears, hugs and stories shared in those moments.

A few days before she died, I experienced a moment I have

cherished my entire life. Although I struggled to see her suffer and didn't like going to the hospital, I had gone to visit her on this particular day. Her room was filled with loved ones as we all sat staring at her struggling to breathe. She seemed unaware of what was going on around her. Suddenly, through her garbled speech, she demanded everyone to leave the room. As we all quickly piled into the hallway, she yelled, "You can stay!" As I turned to look, I realized she was pointing at me. I don't know if she knew who I was in that moment, but she needed me. We needed each other. I sat with her for quite a while, just the two of us while I held her hand, listening to her short and shallow breaths. We never said a word. We didn't need to. I'm so grateful for that moment in time. It provided me with a peace that words can't explain. Perhaps it allowed her to let go and finally be free.

There are times in our lives that are beautifully ordained by God to imprint unforgettable moments on our heart. Sometimes they are big life events, other times they are simple yet profound instances that change us and bring peace to our souls. God can use the most joyful and the most tragic of circumstances to fill you with His love and peace. Even if no words are spoken, these moments in time leave a mark on our lives that stay with us forever. Embrace these gifts from God and use them to learn, grow and impact the world around you.

Today's Prayer:
Lord, thank you for the moments you shower me with throughout my life that teach me to appreciate the gifts of love all around. Help me to recognize these moments and learn from them, so I continue to grow into the person you created me to be.

5
No Words Required

> *For God alone, O my soul, wait in silence, for my hope is from Him.*
>
> *– Psalm 62:5*

My grandfather wasn't the warmest and most compassionate individual – that department was left to my grandmother. Although he selflessly provided for his family, children and grandchildren, he was a man of few words. And if he did speak, let's just say he had no filter. He drank beer and wine – a lot of it. He made it clear he was raised during the Great Depression and that "money doesn't grow on trees." Growing up, I honestly can't remember him telling me he loved me, hugging me or giving me a kiss. I knew he loved me, he just didn't express it very well.

I vividly remember the day my mom died. I had been at the hospital with her but had gone home – unable to face the reality in front of me. I heard my grandparents' car pull up – holding my breath listening to every step as they approached. It seemed like an eternity. As they walked through the front door, they didn't need to speak any words. She was gone. The room started to spin and I lost my breath. I somehow managed to walk to my room in a haze and shut the door. As I sat on the edge of my bed sobbing, my door slowly opened and my grandfather appeared in my doorway with tears streaming down his face. It's the first time I remember him crying. Cancer is ugly. Death doesn't make sense, especially to a 15-year-old teenager. But in that moment, it was my grandfather who held me in his arms while we cried together for what seemed like hours. He never said a word – he didn't need to. His act of kindness and love provided me with indescribable comfort and taught me a lesson I've carried with me my entire life.

I recently heard my friend and mentor Tammy Hotsenpiller

say something I'll never forget – simple answers to complex questions are usually wrong. Sometimes there are no words that can be spoken in times of tragedy and suffering. I've learned in these moments, you can provide beautiful peace to a hurting soul simply by being there. Find ways to reach out to people who need to be loved, even if you are speechless. Maybe they need someone to cry with them. Perhaps, they just need your silent presence, giving them peace with the reminder that they are not alone. Fight the urge to provide the answers we all desperately want in times of uncertainty. Instead, just be there. Don't come with a sermon; simply being present is enough.

When there are no words, rest in God's gracious arms.

When there are no words, your prayers are still heard.

When there are no words, you can find peace in the silence.

When there are no words, God still speaks and loves.

When there are no words, choose to still be present.

Today's Prayer:
Lord, use me even when I have no words to speak. Help me push through my insecurities so I can be confident and rest in your eternal love, even in the silence. Give me the courage to simply be present for the people in my life.

──── 6 ────
An Eternal Bond

> *I will be your Father, and you will be my sons and daughters, says the LORD Almighty.*
>
> *– 2 Corinthians 6:18*

I never really knew my biological father. The last memory I have of him from my childhood is from when I was quite little, maybe five years old. Growing up knowing my father didn't want to be part of my life or didn't know how to be part of it, had an impact on me. I didn't understand why my other friends had fathers and I didn't. My mother was dying, and

I was left to pick up the pieces. For the first few years after their separation, he periodically took me out for dinners and weekends, but those ended pretty quickly. He would call every couple of years and tell my mom he wanted to see me, but he never came. For years I waited for him, and he never showed up.

Eventually, my mother remarried the man who God had predestined to be my dad. I was eight years old and stood proudly with my mother and new dad on their wedding day. He was and still is a beautiful example of a father to me even if we aren't blood. Although I moved away from him after my mother died to live with my mother's family, he never stopped being my dad.

A few months before I graduated from high school, my family and I were eating brunch at a restaurant after church. It was Easter Sunday, 1988. I was with my grandparents, aunts, uncles and cousins from my mother's side of the family. It's funny how God works in the most unsuspecting places. Standing in the buffet line with my aunt Elaine while scooping up refried beans, rice and enchiladas, she suddenly grabbed me, hugged me and started sobbing. It was pretty awkward and I was very confused. She abruptly turned me around where I was face-to-face with an older man who looked like he just saw a ghost. "DO YOU KNOW WHO THIS IS?" she screamed at the man right in the middle of the buffet line. He nodded his head in acknowledgement as tears rolled down his face. It was my father! No words were spoken and we simply walked away. A few minutes later, he came to our table. My grandfather stood up like a grizzly bear protecting his baby cub. The man standing in front of me was shaking, crying and rambled on with what seemed to be an attempted apology for a lifetime of mistakes. I was able to speak with him for a few minutes and he asked if I would be willing to have dinner with him. I did meet him for dinner – it was uncomfortable for me, but I'm glad I did.

A few months later, he showed up at my high school graduation with his new wife – again awkward. However, what I remember most was the look on my dad's face. I can't imagine what he was feeling in that moment to see another man claiming to be my father, simply walking into my graduation after all of those years. I clung to my dad's side. In that moment, I wanted to scream out, "YOU ARE MY DAD!" I just stayed by him. I never saw my biological father after that day. A few years later, I was notified that he passed away.

We are not defined by what anyone else says about us. My biological father simply didn't know how to be a father to me. I came to realize I was okay without him – I forgave him. I learned we are children of the most-high God who is wild about us. Our eternal father will NEVER leave or abandon us. Go to God with your deepest secrets, dreams and wishes. He desires a relationship with you. He loves you just the way you are, regardless of how many times you mess up. That's the stunning beauty of the cross. Jesus sets you free from your sins so you don't need to live with guilt, shame or fear. You don't need to earn His love by living a life that is worthy of His love. He pours His grace out and covers your imperfections and mistakes, regardless of them. Even if you experience broken and harmful relationships here on earth, you are loved by your father in heaven.

I'm so glad I was finally able to see my adoring and loving heavenly Father give me another earthly father to love, guide and mentor me ... and that is more than enough. Life doesn't always go in the direction we think it will. Relationships wither while new and unexpected ones bloom. Embrace God's unique and unsuspecting gifts, even if they don't look like what everyone else has.

Today's Prayer:
Lord, thank you for loving me and for the promise I have in you. When I am feeling lost and alone, lead me back to you, my eternal Father who will never leave me.

7
From Runaway to Revival

> *Therefore do not be ashamed of the testimony about our Lord, nor of me his prisoner, but share in suffering for the gospel by the power of God.*
>
> *– 2 Timothy 1:8*

I was a pretty good kid growing up. Good grades and very active in sports. I didn't have time to get into trouble. For several months after my mom's death, I held it together pretty well. I literally went back to my life like nothing had happened, numb and in complete denial of what had just occurred. I didn't know it at the time, but I hadn't grieved for her. It wasn't until the following year that my world began to crumble all around me.

I didn't understand why I was so angry – but I was enraged. This eventually seeped into my everyday life and started impacting my friendships, grades and the relationship with my dad. My anger led to new friends who introduced me to drugs and a totally different lifestyle. At first, I felt free from the pain I couldn't shake. Eventually, I ran away from home and stayed with friends or slept in my car. This went on for months. I felt invincible and untouchable – no one was going to tell me what to do. Eventually, I dropped out of high school.

My dad had called the police and reported me missing along with his car. I knew I had to lay low because the police were looking for me – the runaway. After my dad found me one evening in the parking lot of a fast food restaurant, I refused to come with him, so he called the police. I ran. I remember it like it was yesterday. I was terrified and escaped into an apartment complex seeking a place to hide. Within minutes, police officers were swarming the entire complex with flashlights. I found an unlocked truck with a camper shell filled with construction equipment. I climbed into the truck bed and submerged myself into the junk that filled the back of the truck. I laid still, breathing slowly, shaking so hard I was convinced the truck must be shaking along with me, all while trying not to draw attention to myself. I remember the flashlights beaming into the truck several times as the police cars drove by over and over again. I felt like I was in an action adventure movie, a movie I didn't want any part of. I stayed hidden for hours. My silence turned into weeping. "What are you doing?" I asked myself. For a moment, I thought about jumping up and asking for help as the police lights flashed over my head – I didn't. Instead, I jumped over the fence of the apartment complex which landed me on the freeway. I walked along the busy freeway in the dark until I got to a payphone and called a friend to come pick me up. I was out of options – no money, no car and no bed to sleep in.

I came up with the brilliant idea to run away to Los Angeles. The lights of Hollywood looked far more glamorous than the beaming police flash lights and the streets I was walking. I was convinced I would figure out a way to support myself, no matter what I needed to do. I hitched a ride to the train station with a small backpack, consisting of all my possessions. To my surprise, when I arrived at the station, there were no trains left for the night. I sunk onto the cold concrete bench, completely broken. After a few minutes, I opened my eyes fixed upon a beautiful starry night, blurred by my relentless tears. Although I had been raised in the church from a young age, I realized I didn't really *know* God. In that moment, I cried out to Him, "God if you're there, I'm listening." He had my attention. I knew I couldn't continue down the road I was on any longer. It's hard to explain what happened next, but I had an overwhelming sense of peace rush across every part of me. It's as if God reached down and covered me with a heavenly blanket, a blanket that calmed my soul and filled me with absolute love. From that moment on, everything changed for me.

A few days later, I snuck back into my dad's house, took the car walked toward the door, the coach stopped and asked me who I was. I told her I was new to the school and that I was a hurdler, a jumper and a sprinter. It was pretty clear she didn't take me seriously and told me the school had one of the league's top hurdlers. In that moment, I knew I was going to prove her wrong.

As the season went along, I slowly climbed the ladder earning a spot in each of my events. I swear she pushed me harder than any of the other athletes on the field. But, I eventually earned her respect. At the end of the season, our school participated in an invitational with all the other schools in the area. The last event of the weekend turned out to be a race that would determine which school would be named league champions that year. It was my event – the hurdles. The winner of the race had already been predicted, and it wasn't me. I was up against some pretty fierce competition, including an undefeated runner from a rival high school with a better personal best time. I don't think anyone contemplated someone could actually beat her. From the start of the race until the last millisecond, I was neck-and-neck with her. As I crossed the finish line, I knew what had just occurred – I pulled off the biggest upset of the year and our school was named league champion. If you haven't seen the movie Rudy, you have to see it. I know it sounds super dramatic, but it's the only way I can describe what happened next. My team lifted me in the air and marched me around. Lifted in the air, I caught a glimpse of my grandparents in the stands jumping up and down. My grandfather was crying – I don't think it was because I won the race – it was so much more than that. I was finally walking on my own again, in fact, I was running.

At the track awards banquet, just before I graduated from high school, my coach talked about each player and handed out a few special awards. She got to the end of the roster in front of hundreds of people and could hardly speak as she announced my name. I received the award for the Most Outstanding Athlete as she told the story of that first day when I walked into the informational meeting. She said she had learned a lot from me and my perseverance and how proud she was to be my coach.

I learned a lot that season ...
- Never give up.
- Don't stay down.
- Push through doubt.
- Try things that might scare you.
- If you fall, get back up and try again.
- You CAN start over and find joy again.

Today's Prayer:
Lord, I believe you will do what you have promised to do and that your love for me is enough. Give me the courage to start over when I feel doubt. I ask the Spirit of God to remove any doubt I have and strengthen me to push forward in love.

9
A New Forever Family

> *Greater love has no one than this: to lay down one's life for one's friends.*
> *– John 15:13*

Graduating from high school was somewhat of a miracle given what I had experienced just a few years before. I decided to enroll at the local junior college but was scared to death. I felt all alone. At 18 years old and without my parents, it was challenging to motivate myself to get up each day and head to class. Somehow, though, I did it. I didn't know it at the time, but God had ordained a lifelong friendship that has brought immense love to my life for nearly 30 years. Steph was the captain of our college cheerleading squad. She was two years older than me and took me under her wing. We became very close that first year of college. We would sit up all night talking and listening to our favorite music. We laughed until we cried, revealed our deepest fears and had the courage to voice our biggest dreams out loud, knowing we were safe with each other.

Steph knew my turbulent past and still loved me unconditionally. She often invited me over to her house where I became very close with her mother, Shirley. Before I knew it, they asked me to move in and we became a family. In a funny way, we all needed each other more than any of us realized. They taught me so much about selfless love. We have seen each other through every twist and turn of our lives since that time. Weddings, babies, graduations, funerals and far away moves that stung. Laughter, tears, hugs and even sitting in silence through unbearable pain. They've been there. I don't know if they will ever fully grasp what they did for me or if I've appropriately thanked them. I walked into college a scared 18-year-old kid unsure of my future, and came out part of an amazing family.

We are called to love others and be a blessing in this world – to live the kind of life Jesus modeled for us. He was constantly loving the unloved when no one else would. He became a presence that couldn't be ignored, pushing into the lives of societal outcasts, refusing to settle for less than selfless love. It's not about memorizing scripture, having a perfect prayer life or converting others; it's about reflecting the love of Jesus in everything we do. It's easy to get stuck in our comfortable lives, avoiding the inconvenience of sacrifice. So much of what we see in this world tells us to worry about ourselves, but true joy comes from giving yourself, even when you don't feel you have the resources, time or patience. When opportunities are put in front of you to be a blessing, you will know it deep down in your spirit. Open up your home, your heart or maybe even your wallet if you can. When faced with the choice to remain stagnant and comfortable, push out and be a blessing to someone. Who knows, you might change the life of a lost teenager and create memories that will last a lifetime.

Today's Prayer:
Lord, thank you for the divine appointments you arrange in my life and for the people you have put into my life that have blessed me beyond measure. Help me to be a blessing in this same way to others who come across my path.

Part Two
POWER

10
Slow Down and Listen

> *Your own ears will hear him.*
> *Right behind you a voice will say,*
> *"This is the way you should go,"*
> *whether to the right or to the left.*
>
> *– Isaiah 30:21*

CANCER? I couldn't help but realize I was nearly the exact same age my mother was when she died when I received my own news. After getting the diagnosis, everything went pretty quickly. Scans, bloodwork, x-rays and oncology appointments. Eventually, I was able to have surgery that left me with an excellent prognosis. The only problem was, because of the surgery, I was unable to have more children. Don't get me wrong, I was blessed with three amazing kids. But, I knew in the depths of my soul we were supposed to have another child.

As I recovered at home in a hospital bed, I sensed an undeniable urge that my husband Craig and I were going to adopt a child. I kept dismissing the idea as complete lunacy. Who would approve *me* to adopt? It didn't make sense. But, the feeling didn't go away and I could no longer ignore it. I found out that putting me on my back in a hospital bed, unable to move and armed with a laptop can be pretty dangerous. Eventually, I ended up on multiple adoption websites and before I knew it, I was on the phone speaking with an adoption agency. After finding out about my diagnosis, they politely advised me that we would never be approved to adopt. There were strict requirements to meet including obtaining a clean bill of health that I wouldn't be able to fulfill. Cancer didn't fit the profile for appropriate adoptive parents. I persisted. I called at least ten agencies, all of them providing me the same resounding, "NO!"

The last call I made changed our family's life forever. I told the agency of my medical condition (as I still laid in a hospital bed in my home) and they said they "might" be able to get approval with a doctor's note stating my prognosis was very good. It was at this point I clued Craig in on the adventure I knew we were about to embark on. He was all in! Within a week, I had already provided the agency with a letter from my doctor. Then, we waited. Fast forward eight months later. We received the call we were approved and that our little girl was waiting for us. Five weeks later we traveled to Ethiopia to meet our sweet little girl for the first time. Looking back, I can truly say I thank God for allowing me to endure cancer. In my crazy, busy life, I might have never slowed down enough to hear Him speaking to me. I was so caught up in checking off my to-do list each day, that I never stopped to listen and contemplate what God was whispering to me.

"And we know that for those who love God all things work together for good, for those who are called according to his purpose" (Romans 8:28).

Sometimes, we need to be shaken up, have the carpet pulled out from underneath us and forced to literally lay on our back to hear God speak. It is in these moments He will speak to us in a still-small voice His sweetest blessings He wants to lavish upon us. It might not feel like it at the time, but somehow God will use your pain to bring about something amazing.

You will look at the world differently and relate to others from a new and compassionate perspective. His love is like a crashing wave we can't outrun, overtaking us with His grace. We just need to slow down and listen.

Today's Prayer:
Lord, I yearn to hear you speak to me each day. When I stray away and don't lean into you, pull me back into your loving embrace and pour out your grace and mercy upon my life so I can hear your loving voice.

11
Community Counts

> *Blessed are those who hunger and thirst for righteousness for they will be filled.*
>
> *– Matthew 5:6*

There's something about eating a meal with people that is truly life-giving. In the fast food world we live in, it's easy to pass by opportunities to spend quality time with friends and family. Over the years, I've come up with countless excuses to avoid having to commit to these moments because I've put my own needs, work schedule and family ahead of other people. I'm sure I missed out on many opportunities to love and simply be in the moment.

We love going out to eat at our favorite restaurants. However, there's something wonderful about having friends and family over and making a home-cooked meal. It's an intimacy that can't be experienced when you are in a public place surrounded by a room full of strangers. We don't do this often enough and it's something I've made a commitment to getting better at. We've had some of the deepest and most life-giving moments sitting in our backyard or at a friend's house, investing in one another. I've laughed until I cried and wept deeply during some of these unforgettable times. Our friends Sheila and Barry have beautifully modeled the importance of investing time in others. They have always had a standing family night each week, even though their children are all grown and some have children of their own. For years, I came up with many excuses as to why such a weekly event would be impossible for our busy family. But, through their model of love, our family has been impacted and now we have family night every Sunday. It's a day I look forward to each week. We create memories that bring immeasurable joy through the simplicity of presence and time.

Put the phone down, check your texts later ... the emails can wait. Take a step of faith each and every day to connect with someone and tell them how important they are. Look them in the eyes so they know they are being heard and loved. Make meaningful time to sit across from a friend, co-worker or family member to invest in them. And when you do, be present with them. Set your busy schedule aside. Find inspiration from others around you. Instead of making a reservation at a local restaurant, make a home-cooked meal or order in and invite friends and family over. You will gain an eternal return on your investment.

Today's Prayer:
Lord, I'm so thankful for the opportunities you put in front of me every day, allowing me to be a blessing to others. Help me to see people in need and encourage me to step out in faith to create community, even when I feel I don't have the time.

12
God's Got This

> *The temptations in your life are no different from what others experience. And God is faithful. He will not allow the temptation to be more than you can stand. When you are tempted, He will show you a way out so that you can endure.*
>
> *– 1 Corinthians 10:13*

"God won't give you more than you can handle!" These are the words typically uttered to you during a crisis when no one knows what to say. When you feel like your heart's been ripped out of your chest, these are NOT comforting words. Plus, it's usually not true, since we won't come out unscathed from every storm. We can't physically and emotionally handle everything that happens to us. Although most of our worst fears will never come true, sometimes we are faced with situations that shake us to our core. In fact, many times we will be tested and stretched far beyond our human capacity and ability to cope, far more than we can handle. There are times in my life where I thought I'd never get through the storm that was overtaking me, but, I did make it through. It's through the most difficult of times, the times when I was at the end of my fraying rope, that I not only learned I couldn't get through it alone – I realized something much more profound – nothing is beyond what God can handle. He is present through it all.

When my first son was a toddler, we noticed his extremely high energy and struggles to maintain acceptable social boundaries with other children. As he grew older and started school, we had our share of parent-teacher conferences. I'll never forget Craig and I sitting in the toddler chairs being grilled by his preschool teacher asking why he kept biting the other children. We looked at each other wondering if we were really expected to have a rational answer to her question. I kept wanting to say, "He's three, are we supposed to reason with him?" By the age of five, we started noticing he would involuntarily tic by twitching his head, sniffing and coughing over and over again. He was drawing attention to himself at school with these tics along with his struggles to maintain his energy and to appropriately socialize with his peers. We felt totally unequipped to help him. We tried everything. Endless doctor's appointments, brain scans and numerous therapies wore all of us down. His teacher was a saint and did everything she could to help him in the classroom, but we soon learned his needs were beyond what any of us could handle without more concrete answers and additional support.

Autism was the last word we expected to hear from his doctor. I was angry. Angry at God that He allowed my son to endure these struggles. Angry I didn't know how to help him. "It's not fair," I found myself repeating over and over again in my head. Will he ever have friends? Will he have to attend a different school? Will he go to college or get married? My mind was bombarded with endless questions driven by fear and irrational thoughts. I remember crying out to God in my selfish pity party demanding, "WHY ME?" I overstayed my pity party for quite a while, but eventually pulled myself up and thrust forward into mommy-mode. We figured out therapies that worked for him and obtained the support from his teachers and school. He even made a few friends. He participated in many sports and excelled in football. We always joked he was such a good football player, because he could run full speed into another human being and tackle them without getting into trouble. Years later, I remember watching him shine on the high school football field as he terrorized the running backs with each tackle. I cried. That night, I found myself on my bruised and tattered knees crying out to God, "WHY HAVE YOU BLESSED ME WITH THIS AMAZING CHILD?" I was overcome with joy and honored to be his mom. It's funny, he's taught me more than I could ever teach him. Acceptance. Joy. Love.

There are situations in our lives that will bring us to our knees, pleading with God. Sometimes, we are unable to deal with life's struggles and tragedies, yet there is no circumstance that God cannot handle. He's the key. He knows the beginning from the end and nothing is a surprise to Him. He's got this! Lean into Him and rest in His unending love. God hears your prayers, even if you can't muster up the words yourself. At the bottom of the deepest pit, He is there. Turn everything over to Him – your fears, anxieties, worries, hopes and dreams. He hears, He listens and He loves. God is enough!

Today's Prayer:
Lord, thank you for allowing me to go through the storm and staying with me through it all. It's in the struggle and the pain that I learn to lean into you and trust you with everything I have.

13
Be Present

> *Now listen, you who say, "Today or tomorrow we will go to this or that city, spend a year there, carry on business and make money." Why, you do not even know what will happen tomorrow. What is your life? You are a mist that appears for a little while and then vanishes.*
>
> *– James 4:13-14*

When my children were little, I loved reading them bedtime stories. I don't think I fully appreciated the countless beautiful moments I experienced just watching their faces as we turned the pages. Eventually, our nighttime ritual turned into them reading to me as they practiced their newly learned reading skills. As they got older, story time became less of a priority and was replaced with baseball practice, dance rehearsals and homework. Time was slipping away and I was desperately grasping to get those moments back. If only I could suspend time and do it all over again.

When my youngest daughter was ten years old, we hardly ever read together any more. I made the decision to buy her a girl's devotional book and asked her if she would read to me every night. Each day has an inspiring message that leads us to a sweet conversation reflecting on what we just read. We started off slow, but before I knew it, we were both looking forward to our nightly lesson. As I watched my daughter read and sometimes giggle her way through some of the funny stories and lessons, I found myself praying that time would stand still so I wouldn't forget that feeling of adoration and love. Each night she comes in to read to me, I've learned to immediately put down whatever I'm doing and be present (this took practice). What I've been most blessed with in these moments, are the conversations that take place after she puts the book down. Snuggling up to me, we talk about her day and I laugh at her silly stories and simply love what we are experiencing in that moment.

When you are too tired to read with your little one, take a deep breath and ask her to read just one more story. When your phone won't stop urging you to check your text messages, choose to turn it off and look your loved one in the eyes when you are with them. Instead of sending that last email, turn off your computer and be present. Deny the urge to take time to create a social media post of the amazing moment you just experienced and simply stay in that moment with no distractions. Then, you will truly live and be present.

Today's Prayer:
Lord, thank you for helping me to embrace the simple moments in life that I can enjoy with my loved ones, free of distractions and totally focused on what truly matters.

14
The Waiting Room

> *Therefore, as God's chosen people, holy and dearly loved, clothe yourselves with compassion, kindness, humility, gentleness and patience.*
>
> *– Colossians 3:12*

We live in a world that expects immediate results. Standard mail is too slow and has been replaced with overnight express. Email has nearly taken the place of mail altogether. We don't even need to leave the comfort of our home to go shopping and can order everything we need online. Text messaging, Snap Chat, Instagram and Twitter plug us into the global chaos of immediacy. We even have the option at our fingertips to FaceTime or Skype people on video to actually see who we are talking to whenever we want at the press of a button. Taking a vacation in your car, peering out the window asking, "ARE WE THERE YET?" is rare and has been replaced with quick flights getting us to our destination in the blink of an eye. Cooking dinner and sitting down at the table has become less and less important. Fast food isn't even fast enough and has double lanes for us to get fed quicker! Library research has been swallowed up by website research sites. Theme parks have fast passes so we can squeeze in more rides and wait less. We are a society who has lost any sense of patience. These advancements have been a huge blessing, yet, I yearn to slow down and rest in the wait.

Over the years, I've sat in many waiting rooms in hopeful anticipation of several friends' newborn babies. The joy filling the room in these moments is almost indescribable. I've also been in the waiting room feeling gut-wrenching anguish, wondering if my loved one would pull through the night. The Bible is filled with people who waited on God through circumstances that seemed impossible ... promises of conceiving children at an old age, the vow to be rescued from exile and the anticipation of God's return to bring us home to heaven. Much can be learned in times of wonder, intrigue and expectation. Persevering through struggle, pain and uncertainty creates strength to carry us throughout a lifetime.

Therefore the LORD waits to be gracious to you, and therefore he exalts himself to show mercy to you. For the LORD is a God of justice; blessed are all those who wait for him" (Isaiah 30:18).

Are you waiting for God to answer a prayer? Does it seem like you've prayed and prayed and nothing is happening? It might not always make sense, but God is present through it all. God is present through the victories. God is present through the fight. God is present through the silence. In fact, He accomplishes some of His best work in the waiting room. Rest in His perfect plan. He will answer all of your prayers in His time. Someday, it will all make sense.

Today's Prayer:
Heavenly Father, help me to slow down in my fast-paced life and truly enjoy the ride. When I don't get the immediate results I'm seeking, help me to see immense value in the wait.

15
Even if the Mountain Doesn't Move

> *Praise be to the God and Father of our Lord Jesus Christ! In his great mercy He has given us new birth into a living hope through the resurrection of Jesus Christ from the dead, and into an inheritance that can never perish, spoil or fade. This inheritance is kept in heaven for you, who through faith are shielded by God's power until the coming of the salvation that is ready to be revealed in the last time.*
>
> *– 1 Peter 1:3-5*

As a Christian, my faith is grounded in the death and resurrection of Jesus Christ; our eternal hope is in Him. We know all of the bumper sticker and coffee cup Bible verses to lift us up when we are down. Of course, there are also countless verses we cling to when life is beautiful. But, what about the times when we are in the deepest depths of despair, unable to pull ourselves out of the sinking sand of grief? Will those verses bring us the same comfort they do when our world is spiraling out of control? Can we still believe what we have always said we believe, when everything we know has been turned upside down?

Over the past few years, I've known several people who have experienced unimaginable pain through the unexpected loss of their spouse or loved ones. I recently heard an amazing woman of faith I know from our community speaking to a group of high school students. She had unexpectedly lost her husband less than two months before and courageously spoke of her faith during her time of unfathomable loss. She talked about how easy it was to speak about the truth of scripture, faith and prayer before her husband had passed away. I was stunned as she stood in front of hundreds of high schoolers and parents and passionately asserted her faith was even stronger now. She talked about how the song "Even If" by Mercy Me was one of her favorite songs and the peace it brings her. I had never heard it before that day, so I went to my phone and pulled up the song and listened to it. The lyrics pierced my soul, challenging me that even if the ground beneath me is giving way and the pain seems too much to bear, I will keep my eyes on Jesus and rest in His promises.

There is a story found in the sixteenth chapter of Acts, where the apostles Paul and Silas were wrongly imprisoned in Philippi, a Roman colony. After being stripped, beaten and shackled, instead of being discouraged, they praised and sang to God. In the face of a frightening and uncertain future, they chose faith in God when the reality all around them looked like God was nowhere to be found. I can't help but wonder what the guards and other inmates must have been thinking, listening to their songs of praise. I love the next part in the story. The text states: "Suddenly there was such a violent earthquake that the foundations of the prison were shaken. At once all the prison doors flew open, and everyone's chains came loose" (Acts 16:26). In the darkness of the midnight hour, amongst the worst of circumstances, Paul and Silas praised and sang to God, opening prison doors and breaking chains. They had an even if faith!

The reality is, we are all going to experience loss. It's not if, but when. My prayer is when we are faced with the worst type of tragedy, we will cling to our hope in Jesus and fully grasp that this world is temporary, but our hope in Him is eternal. The storms will come, but we will stand firm on the rock of God's eternal promise. He will give us the strength to move forward each day so we can fully grasp His promise of eternal life with Him in heaven. Even if this world doesn't make sense, even if

He doesn't move the mountain and even if He doesn't prevent something that rocks our world, He is King and His promises are true.

Today's Prayer:
Lord, thank you for the eternal hope we have in Jesus Christ. Strengthen me when the storms of life overcome me and carry me through to victory!

16
The Day That Changed Me

> *So if there is any encouragement in Christ, any comfort from love, any participation in the Spirit, any affection and sympathy, complete my joy by being of the same mind, having the same love, being in full accord and of one mind.*
>
> *– Philippians 2:1-2*

Several years ago, I was asked to speak at an event. It included hundreds of women from a homeless shelter; many of them were struggling with drug abuse and were coming to hear words of encouragement. As I approached the podium with my polished pre-written speech on notecards, perfectly pressed suit, curled hair and meticulously applied makeup, I took a moment to look into the eyes of these women looking back at me in disbelief. I had spoken many times to different types of women's groups, but this one was different. These women were broken. I could see it in their eyes – a distrust for me as they were convinced I could never offer them any hope. They were not having any of it; their arms were crossed, they rolled their eyes and some women even walked out. What could I possibly say? How in the world could *I* relate to them and provide them hope? Something told me to scratch my speech and simply speak to this hurting group from my heart.

I started off by asking the question, "I bet you think I have it all together standing up here in this nice suit right?" I was onto something, based on their reaction. In that moment, I decided to be completely and totally vulnerable with a group of strangers. I told them about growing up watching my mother struggle with a terminal illness most of my life, being abandoned by my biological father, losing my mother to cancer, becoming so deeply depressed I didn't want to live, dropping out of high school, running away from home, running from the police and turning to drugs and the wrong crowd. I told them everything, I didn't hold back. I went on to describe how I climbed out of the deepest despair and pulled myself up one day at a time. How I enrolled back in high school, attended community college then transferred to a four-year university, and eventually on to law school. I found love and a family.

I'm not sure what these women learned on that day or if they felt encouraged, but I was. By the end of my speech, most of them were standing in line to hug me while we all cried. Two women told me they had decided to go back to college after hearing my story. They said, "If you can do it, we can do it!" It was a profound moment in my life. I left the event filled with joy, enthusiasm and hope. I pray the women I met that day did too. It would've been easy to stick with my script, fearful my story didn't really matter. But my story did matter. We all have stories that matter. God allows our story to unfold in unanticipated ways to teach us and inspire others. On that day, I learned to push back fear, embrace the fullness of my genuine story and speak from a true place of love. I woke up that morning prepared to change the lives of women – but it was them who changed me.

Today's Prayer:
Heavenly Father, give me the strength to push through fear and be genuine to who I truly am. Illuminate opportunities for me to help others and love them even when I don't feel I have the skills and ability to do so.

17
Ignore and Believe

> *Finally, brothers and sisters, whatever is true, whatever is noble, whatever is right, whatever is pure, whatever is lovely, whatever is admirable—if anything is excellent or praiseworthy—think about such things.*
>
> *– Philippians 4:8*

Our world constantly floods us with information, social media alerts and commercials telling us where we can find true happiness. Fashion dos and don'ts, parenting advice, hairstyles, fancy vacations and expensive cars top the list. It's easy to be defined by who the world says we should be. The more we strive to obtain earthly possessions and accolades, the more of them we want or think we need. But guess what. It will never be enough. Have you ever noticed the one thing you just had to have, the one thing that would make your life complete ... didn't? Pretty soon, you start believing what the world is saying about you – that you won't find true joy without accumulating more stuff. It's exhausting! For years, I was caught in this exact web of seeking what the world had to offer me. It took me a while to grasp and I experienced a lot of tough lessons, but I eventually learned that what the world had for me would never be enough. I realized I would continue to chase the uncatchable wind of progress my entire life if I didn't refocus my attention on what truly mattered.

Instead of trying to be someone the world says you should be or obtaining the things this world has to offer, focus on what is true, beautiful and lovely. Focus on who God says you are. Focus on the love Jesus displayed and calls us to spread abundantly. Live a life of love, reflecting the life of Jesus and you will find fulfillment that can't be bought. We must learn to reject the things that tell us to be something we are not and fully grasp and believe what God says about us. Rest in the beautiful simplicity of who you are, right where you are in this moment. We don't need more of this world, we need more of God. We need more love. God will fill every void this world will never come close to filling.

Reject what the world says about you ...
  Reject self-doubt.
  Reject negativity.
  Reject the urge to be distracted from what truly matters.
  Reject the constant social media alerts.
  Reject another's displaced anger upon you.

Believe what God says about you. You are ...
  Loved.
  Adored.
  Made in His image.
  A child of God.
  Liberated.
  Fully able.
  Completely equipped.

Today's Prayer:
Lord, thank you for creating me just the way I am. I am unique and perfectly equipped for the mission you have called me to. I fully grasp I am your daughter, I am loved and I am all you created me to be.

18
Life is Precious

> *In a flash, in the twinkling of an eye, at the last trumpet. For the trumpet will sound, the dead will be raised imperishable, and we will be changed.*
>
> *– 1 Corinthians 15:52*

There are some moments that are etched in our memories for a lifetime, certain people that touch our lives and leave an imprint on our hearts forever. The last time I spoke with my grandmother was one of those moments. What I remember most is her laugh. She was watching our daughter Taylor who was 15 months old at the time. I had called to check on her and let my grandmother know we were on our way to their house. She told me about the funny things Taylor was saying and I could hear the smile in her voice just talking with her. As we hung up the phone, I remember thinking how blessed I was to have her in my life, especially because my mother wasn't able to be there. Our little girl brought her so much joy.

Thirty minutes later, as we pulled onto the street entering my grandparent's neighborhood, we were faced with fire trucks, police cars and an ambulance. We could see their house for at least a quarter of a mile before we could actually get there. The 30 seconds it took to get there felt like an eternity. Craig drove what seemed like 80 miles per hour to get to their house as I screamed, "NO, NO, NO!" I flew out of the car while it was still moving as we landed the truck on the front lawn. I was terrified Taylor may have been hurt. I quickly switched gears and assumed something had happened to my grandfather since he had many health issues for years. My heart and mind were racing as I frantically tried to navigate my way through the police officers, paramedics and neighbors in the driveway. Time seemed to stand still in that moment as I tried to push through the fog of confusion. It was then that I saw my grandfather sitting in the driveway crying. I was in a haze, unable to catch my breath, looking around as the world surrounding me started to spin like an accelerating merry-go-round. Somehow, my gaze landed on a gardener who was holding our sweet Taylor. I never for a moment thought it would be my grandmother laying on the living room floor, but there she was. The paramedics tried to revive her while I watched in horror. My grandmother was rushed to the hospital, but it was too late.

> *"So teach us to number our days that we may get a heart of wisdom" (Psalm 90:12).*

We don't know when we will be called home. Cherish the moments you have been given and live life to its fullest. Love deeply, forgive often and tell people how much they mean to you. Speak life into others. Find time to do life with friends and loved ones with no agenda. Time is the best gift you can ever give. It can't be bought, yet it's more valuable than any material item you own. Time invested in others fosters beautiful relationships that will lead to a lifetime of joy. Find time to love. Life is truly precious.

Today's Prayer:
Lord, thank you for the amazing people who you have placed in my life. Help me to appreciate them, spend time with them and show them how deeply they are loved.

— 19 —
I'm Here

> *Clap your hands, all you nations; shout to God with cries of joy.*
>
> *– Psalm 47:1*

When my youngest daughter Gracie was in kindergarten, I met with her teacher towards the end of the year. She was a pretty young kindergartner that year and after speaking with her teacher, we had decided she would enroll in kindergarten for a second time the following school year. Most of my meetings with her teacher that year were about Gracie's funny stories, short attention span and inability to control her socialization and talking. During the last week of school, I was talking to her teacher and she asked me with a tone that meant I must already know the answer to the question, "Do you know what Gracie does every day when she arrives to my classroom?" I braced myself for what I was about to hear and no, I had no idea what she did each day. She went on to explain that every morning, Gracie would open the door of the classroom and boldly announce to all who cared to hear, "I'M HERE!" This was followed by a fairly dramatic double arm motion like she was on stage and ready to perform for a crowd of people. Her teacher had the biggest smile on her face as she told me the story. I wasn't surprised by what I heard at all. At the age of twelve, Gracie still has that same zest for life, joy and spunk about her every day. It's infectious!

Jesus walked the earth and loved everyone around Him, no matter what their circumstance may have been. He used every opportunity to teach others about love and compassion. He sought out the sick, the orphan, the widow, the outcast and the marginalized, simply loving them as they were. His untethered love filled others with joy. Living a life of joy starts with love. Without love, there can be no joy. Jesus' model of love is something we should continue to be inspired by, which always leads to a life of joy.

Do you ever have those days where you can barely lift your head off the pillow to drag yourself out of bed? I do! On certain days, I find myself dragging through the day needing a second cup of coffee. We don't need to burst through every door we walk through and announce our presence. But, if we channel just a bit of enthusiasm and joy, even when we feel we can't muster up a simple smile, others will notice and we will lighten the atmosphere everywhere we go. Be an inspiration of love. Joy is contagious. Spread it abundantly!

Today's Prayer:
Lord, help me spread joy everywhere I go today. When I'm feeling discouraged and tired, encourage me to focus on the amazing gifts in my life you have lavished upon me, so that others can see you in my life and feel your love through me.

20
Hurry Up & Slow Down

> *My dear brothers and sisters, take note of this: Everyone should be quick to listen, slow to speak and slow to become angry.*
>
> *– James 1:19*

Like most families, when our kids were younger, we filled every moment of our day with some sort of activity – sports, dance, parties and other events. Trying to maintain a clean house, spotless rooms, clean dishes and laundry was next to impossible. I was always rushing ... everywhere, "Let's go, let's go, let's go!" As I was barking my morning command at my youngest daughter one morning trying to get out the door, I saw a look in her eyes as she closed the door to her room and hustled down the stairs. It was a look that said, "Don't look in my room." So naturally, I did, and yes, it was a total mess. I was tempted to call her back up and have her clean it up, but something stopped me. I realized we had been so busy, we hardly had any time to just breathe, relax and be – let alone keep a perfectly clean room. I had become so focused on where we were going each day, rushing to get to each activity, that I wasn't enjoying the ride to get there. I didn't have her come back up and clean her room that day; it stayed messy for a few days. And that's okay.

I've learned some of the most unforgettable moments are found in the simplicity of life, the in-between moments that can't be scheduled. If we rush through life and don't slow down to breathe in the beauty all around us, we miss opportunities to enjoy simply being present. I started taking small steps to reduce the amount of activities our family was participating in. I became conscious of my hurry up attitude and started to tame it. Having a perfectly kept house became less important than our quality of life. Instead, I made sure to stop and look each of my children in their eyes each day and tell them how amazing they are and how much I love them. Making sure my kids tried out for every team their friends did and saying "yes" to every opportunity became less and less important. While there are times we need to keep a schedule and arrive on time to our commitments, there are many instances where we can simply slow down.

If you must hurry ...
 Hurry up to love.
 Hurry up to give.
 Hurry up to listen.
 Hurry up to forgive.
 Hurry up to appreciate what truly matters.

Perhaps we need to hurry up to slow down too. Life is passing by and before you know it, that moment of time will slip away. Seize these beautiful moments today. Slow down ...
 Slow down to listen to your child breathing as they sleep.
 Slow down to watch your children play.
 Slow down and read a book just because.
 Slow down and take a walk with no agenda.
 Slow down and tell your loved ones how precious they are to you every day.
 Slow down and love!

Today's Prayer:
Lord, thank you for the amazing gifts you have provided me. Help me to slow down and simply appreciate what I have and love the people in my life each day.

21
An Appointment with Destiny

> Trust in the LORD with all your heart; do not depend on your own understanding. Seek his will in all you do, and he will show you which path to take.
>
> – Proverbs 3:5-6

When we were first married, Craig and I lived in a small condominium. It was perfect for our family of three. But, we always dreamed of living in a bigger house and loved walking through model homes, imagining we would one day be able to buy a house and fill it with children. There was a particular neighborhood we fell in love with, but it was way out of our price range. However, we were dreamers and never dismissed the idea. We would visit the model homes in that community sometimes every weekend, getting lost in the beautiful view, decorating ideas and praying one day we would live in that neighborhood. One of the model homes was our favorite. On most days, we would skip all of the other houses and walk straight to that particular model. We must have spent hours in that one home, playing house and dreaming. After a few years, they eventually sold all of the homes in the neighborhood, including our favorite model, halting our sometimes weekly visits.

Several years later, we were finally in a position to buy a home and started looking. Of course, we had always dreamed of moving into our favorite neighborhood and we loved the layout of that one model. We knew it was a long shot to find a home in the neighborhood with that particular layout, but we were praying for it. One day, I was driving my daughter's friend home after a Girl Scout meeting and she told me I needed to drop her off at her grandparent's home. I had never been there. Before I knew it, we were entering that same neighborhood. I felt an immediate sense of nostalgia since we had been in the model homes so many times. With each turn, I told the girls the story of that neighborhood and our dream of someday moving there. I was stunned when she pointed to her grandparent's house, "It's that one," she said. Wouldn't you know it, it was that same model home Craig and I had spent so many hours walking through and praying for. I couldn't help myself and when her grandmother opened the door, I belted out, "I've been in your home so many times!" I'm sure I scared her at first, but then I explained what I was talking about. She asked if I wanted to come in, and of course I accepted. I felt like I was home as I walked around the house remembering our many visits. Jokingly, I said, "If you're ever interested in selling, you've got a buyer." She said, "Funny you should say that, my husband just got a job offer out of state and we are seriously thinking of moving." I was stunned. We ended up buying that house and it was never on the market. We not only got the layout we wanted, we literally bought the exact home we had walked through, prayed over and dreamed about for so many years. Only God!

Don't ever stop praying and dreaming for what God has put on your heart. Sometimes, we don't see our prayers being answered as quickly as we'd like, so we get frustrated. But, God has everything in control and planned out, even to the smallest detail. He will orchestrate each small step for you as you trust, pray and have faith. It might not always end up exactly as you had planned, but if you trust in God and take his lead, you will end up where you are supposed to be. Don't get discouraged, but instead, keep dreaming and pushing forward in faith. Your victory is just around the corner. God leads us to knock on the doors that will change our future and allow our dreams to come true. It's amazing to look back and see His hand all over our lives, like a beautiful puzzle coming together. Most of the time, it doesn't make sense when we are still waiting for our prayers to be answered. Little moments like walking through a model home 50 times don't really mean much. But when you step back and see the beautiful mosaic God's walked through with you, it is simply stunning. Everything finally makes sense.

Today's Prayer:
Lead me Lord, show me where to be you in the world today. Guide all of my steps and allow me to see the world as you see it, through the eyes of love.

22
Picture Perfect

> Not that I have already obtained it or have already become perfect, but I press on so that I may lay hold of that for which also I was laid hold of by Christ Jesus.
>
> *– Philippians 3:12*

I absolutely love receiving Christmas cards in the mail from our friends and family each year. Reading about everyone's adventures and seeing how the kids are growing brings me such delight. However, for my family, obtaining the perfect family photo has always been next to impossible. One of my kids was always crying, hitting someone or walking out of the frame asserting they would not be in the picture.

Several years ago, Craig and I along with our four children were vacationing in Maui. I had the brilliant idea that we would obtain an award-winning Christmas photo while we were there. After hours of attempting to capture the perfect image of our family, we had hundreds of pictures to choose from. The only problem was that in each photo, one of the kids was either crying, angry or looking in a different direction. Even better, there were many images of Craig and I "talking" to the kids, trying to convince them to look at the camera in the middle of their temper tantrum. Then, there's my favorite group of shots of me running to make the picture after setting the self-timer on the camera, only to get several perfect shots of my backside! Frustrated, I marched my family to the shopping center next door where I had seen a photography stand with endless amazing family photos. I quickly slapped down my credit card and told the photographer our sob story. Ultimately, we ended up with a picture of the six of us on the beach at sunset, all matching in white. To make it more impressive, we are all jumping in the air in unison as if to express we were jumping with joy! I still laugh when I look at that photo, because I know what we went through to get it! I know the story behind it. That picture is prominently placed in our living room as the centerpiece of our home.

I've learned to embrace the craziness of my family and enjoy the beautiful chaos of life. I know when I view pictures on social media, there is an untold story behind it I cannot see. I've learned it's okay to not be okay. Being honest about our imperfections and faults brings about a genuineness that can't be manufactured. I think back on that day in Maui and my heart leaps with joy. Not because everything went as planned, in fact, far from it! It reminds me of the deep love I have for my nutty, funny, sarcastic, loving and crazy family. And that is perfect to me!

Today's Prayer:
Lord, help me to accept and enjoy my imperfections so I can truly grasp what is important. Help me to be love, acceptance and genuineness in a world telling us we should be something we are not. Let me be love.

23
Time with God

> *But when you pray, go into your room, close the door and pray to your Father, who is unseen. Then your Father, who sees what is done in secret, will reward you.*
>
> *– Matthew 6:6*

It's easy to get lost in our busy schedules and forget to take time for ourselves. Pressures of being the best wife, mother, daughter or friend can cause us to lose sight of what is truly important. If we aren't careful, we find ourselves competing for the invisible "Woman of the Year" award. For years, I would rush through my day, getting the kids up and off to school, working a full day, attending dance competitions and never missing a football game. Eventually, my crazy schedule started to catch up with me and I was feeling stressed and anxious. I knew something had to give. I needed a shift in my life so I could feel true peace and trust in God's plan.

Although we have attended church regularly since we were married, I wasn't setting aside time each day to focus on reading the Bible, pray and reflect. Don't get me wrong, I had read the Bible several times, front to back. Nevertheless, I hadn't retained most of what I read. I was simply going through the motions. I would read it when I had time, maybe once or twice a week at the most. I prayed at night and usually fell asleep mid-prayer. I didn't journal to reflect what God was putting on my heart. I was merely checking off items on my list that showed I was a good person: Attend church – check. Read the Bible – check. Pray – check (sort of). Nothing changed. I was so frustrated and continued to feel a sense something was missing. After hearing a sermon about the power of prayer and journaling, I knew I had to make a change. That day, I made a commitment to take at least one hour each morning to spend quality time with God. That daily commitment has changed me.

> *"Listen to my voice in the morning, LORD.*
> *Each morning I bring my requests to you*
> *and wait expectantly" (Psalm 5:3).*

Many days, I spend more than an hour with God, getting lost in His presence. Of course, there are days when I can't spend the time I'd like with God, but that's okay. I get back on track the next day. I am a new woman with an amazing sense of peace, love and focus.

People ask me all the time, "What's your secret?" If I could give only ONE piece of advice that will change your life forever, it would be to take time EVERY day to spend with God. Really spend time with Him, reading His word, listening to podcasts, sermons, journaling and praying. The key is to create a plan that works for you. Your entire life will have a new focus, your thoughts will align with God's, He will open doors no one can shut and the Holy Spirit will become alive and active within you. You will start to hear from God and feel His presence throughout each day. It's a powerful way to live. Will you take this step of faith and commit to spending time with Him every day? I hope so! Time with God is food for your soul.

Today's Prayer:
Lord, I long to spend time with you and hear your voice. When my day ahead seems daunting, fill me with peace and focus to choose you before anything or anyone else.

—— 24 ——
A Beautiful Song

> *Consider it pure joy, my brothers and sisters, whenever you face trials of many kinds, because you know that the testing of your faith produces perseverance.*
>
> *– James 1:2-3*

When Craig and I traveled to Ethiopia in 2007 to adopt our daughter Gracie, we saw things I'll never be able to erase from my mind. The devastation, poverty and disease were astonishing. Driving through the streets filled with homeless, hurting and sick children was too much for us to bear. We were constantly in tears. The orphanage where she was living didn't look like the rest of the country we had seen. It was painted in beautiful, bright colors, filled with love and laughter.

On our last day in Ethiopia, we spent several hours at the orphanage with Gracie and the other children who were waiting to be adopted. Craig played in a pick-up soccer game with a group of children, while I sat inside playing peek-a-boo and reading with several toddlers in the nursery. Just before we left for the airport, a group of three boys (about nine or ten years old) asked about the iPod I had. They didn't know what it was. I gave it to them and played music. Their faces lit up as they passed the earphones back and forth to each other. They asked us if they could sing a song for my husband Craig and I. Of course, we agreed. The moments that ensued after are etched on our hearts forever. The three boys proceeded to sing "Jesus Loves the Little Children" at the top of their lungs. We wept. They continued to sing song after song, glorifying God and exuding an infectious joy. It didn't make sense. These were children living in an orphanage, dreaming of being part of a forever family. Many of them had been there for several months. Yet, there they were, singing from the depths of their soul with joy they could barely contain. We were so touched by their resolute joy and love despite their circumstance. It was infectious.

Most days, I fully grasp the amazing life God has given me. However, there are times when my heart is heavy with the stresses of life, and fear creeps in taking over my thoughts. I often reflect on our trip to Ethiopia and the moment those three little boys changed us. It is a memory that brings me back to joy. I've learned to appreciate the simple things and accept that life can be hard. No, we won't live perfect lives by any stretch of the imagination, and that's okay. Our children won't always make the best choices, get straight A's or follow a perfect path. We could get a frightening health report, have to manage threatened finances or even watch relationships become jeopardized. But, we can still choose to live with joy, even when there is a storm brewing all around us. Only then can we truly understand we have been blessed beyond measure. Take time to rest in the beautiful simplicity of life, even if it starts with a simple song.

Today's Prayer:
Lord, help me to appreciate the blessings all around me, even when I'm filled with fear due to circumstances beyond my

control. Help me to choose joy each and every day.

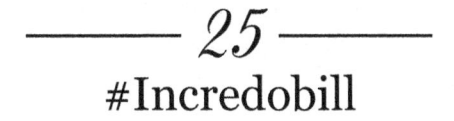

25
#Incredobill

> *For I am convinced that neither death nor life, neither angels nor demons, neither the present nor the future, nor any powers, neither height nor depth, nor anything else in all creation, will be able to separate us from the love of God that is in Christ Jesus our Lord.*
>
> *– Romans 8:38-39*

Bill was the kind of man who you would never forget, even if you met him for only a minute. He was full of life, had no filter, was goofy, the center of attention and had the biggest heart. That was Bill! Craig and I met Bill and his wife Katherine nearly 20 years ago through our children's school. We became close friends. Through the years, we moved neighborhoods and didn't spend as much time with them. But, when we did see them, it was as if no time had gone by at all. Bill always made me feel like I was the only person in the room. I'm sure he made everyone feel this way. When he asked how I was, he really wanted to know. When he talked about his family, you could see sincere love and adoration in his heart. Bill was genuine. Memories of backyard barbeques (Bill actually singed off his eyebrows and the front part of his hairline once) birthday parties and church events are moments I will forever cherish.

In the fall of 2016, Bill started feeling sick. Within a few weeks, he was diagnosed with stage IV esophageal cancer. Unbeknownst to most of our community, several doctors informed him he only had a few months to live and probably wouldn't make it to Christmas. It was September. Bill realized his mission on this earth had changed and he met this new challenge courageously. Even with a terminal diagnosis, Bill never relented his loving, infectious and bigger-than-life personality. He made everyone else feel better about his prognosis. He was an amazing husband, father and friend, and although he continued to fight the odds given to him, he left a beautiful legacy for his family and our entire community to witness. Bill died ten months after his diagnosis, surrounded by family and friends. He taught us how to live in the face of overwhelming heartbreak and how to pass on with grace. Along the way, he brought countless people to know and accept Jesus as their Lord and savior.

The way Bill lived and died has changed me. I have been forever impacted by the courage and grace he showed in the face of death. No, he wasn't a superhero, he was so much more. Bill taught me several life-changing lessons I'll never forget:

Live each day like it will be your last.

Find something you're thankful for every day.

Love deeply.

Be authentic.

Spend quality time with the ones you love.

Allow yourself to be inconvenienced.

Forgive often.

Choose joy.

Today's Prayer:
Heavenly father, thank you for creating me in your image and for giving me breath to breathe each day. Help me to appreciate the people in my life and express my love to them. Today, I choose joy!

26
Slave No More

> *Now you are no longer a slave but God's own child. And since you are His child, God has made you His heir.*
>
> *– Galatians 4:7*

So often, we define ourselves by our circumstances. When the storms of life come, and they will, many times we can only see what is directly in front of us. A frightening health report, financial strain, loss of a loved one, a child who is struggling or a relationship that has ended, can all paralyze us in fear. When our world is crumbling around us, we can easily get swept away by worry, anger and grief. We forget, many times the situation is only temporary. I've met many people that have had terrible things happen to them decades ago, who have never been able to move beyond it. They continue to talk about the situation like it occurred yesterday, overwhelmed by what occurred. This type of mindset can be incredibly damaging to you and those around you. If you aren't careful, you can end up becoming a slave to your situation and become defined by it.

When I was a teenager, I felt like I was under water, unable to catch my breath, sinking deeper and deeper into despair. I felt like I couldn't catch a break. Everywhere I turned, all I could see was loss. I came to accept the fact I was abandoned, unloved and a victim. Of course, none of these beliefs were true. But, I had become a slave to what was occurring around me and couldn't see past my circumstances. The deeper I fell into my world of pain, the more I felt I deserved it. I justified horrible things were happening to me because I had made poor decisions and was therefore being punished.

Eventually, I learned I was a child of God made in His glorious image. In a moment of surrender, God plucked me out of the muck and the mire, brushed me off and called me daughter, loved and adored. He never let me go.

"For we know that our old self was crucified with him so that the body ruled by sin might be done away with, that we should no longer be slaves to sin" (Romans 6:6).

When you are able to fully grasp God is crazy about you and you were made for an amazing purpose, only then can you be released from the chains that enslave you. Only then will you be able to jump into your future, the future God designed for you. Watch and see His miracles rain down all over you. You will go from ...

Slave to saved.

Slave to surrendered.

Slave to sanctified.

Slave to salvation.

Today's Prayer:
Lord, if there are any burdens or chains that enslave me with fear, worry and regret, I break them today. I release everything holding me back from being all you called me to be.

27
Unshakable Identity

> *A good person produces good things from the treasury of a good heart, and an evil person produces evil things from the treasury of an evil heart. What you say flows from what is in your heart.*
>
> *– Luke 6:45*

I am a wife, mother, friend, daughter, sister, niece, student, leader, writer, speaker and attorney. I've got lots of titles, we all do. Some of them are pretty fancy, and I'm proud of them! Nonetheless, far too often we live our lives rattling off our resume, seeking joy grounded in the identity the world gives us. The way we live can easily be seen through our words and actions, which are a direct reflection of where our heart is. Words can build up and words can bless. But, words can also hurt and words can destroy. Our words reveal our hearts. When we are grounded in the truth of this world and defined by it, we will never be satisfied. Seeking more and trying to be better than everyone else won't bring gratification. More titles, more money, more awards and more opportunities to show how amazing WE are gets us nowhere.

One of my best friends is incredibly bright and has too many degrees to count. Since earning her PhD a few years ago, she is usually referred to as Dr. Dani Wilson. On several occasions, I've tried convincing her she should refer to me as Dr. Dani, given I earned my Juris Doctor in law school (I have yet to persuade her). Our group of friends has a running joke – whenever they see the two of us together, they refer to her as "doctor" constantly just to bug me. It drives me nuts! But, Dani isn't defined by her degrees, title or positions – she's defined by love. When you meet her (all jokes aside), she's one of the most kind, gracious and humble human beings I know. Strip away all the degrees, and you are left with a woman filled with love and compassion.

When the storms of life come, our titles are stripped away and our relationships fail, we will be a ship without an anchor living in chaos and seeking rescue. When we are only focused on ourselves and the titles we live by here on this earth, it can become difficult to celebrate others around us. We may find ourselves feeling jealous when we see other people fulfill the things we've dreamed of instead of celebrating them. However, when we find our joy and identity in the God who created us in His image, instead of this world, we are truly free to be who we are and simply love and be loved. It's rather freeing, really. Of course, we should seek to grow, dream and enjoy our accomplishments, but, the key is to remain focused and grounded in the one who created us. There is no room for envy, jealousy and anger when our hearts are fixed upon Him. Even when life doesn't go the way we planned, our kids act up, we lose a job, we get sick or someone we know accomplishes things we have eagerly dreamed of and hoped for, we can genuinely celebrate them and rejoice in their gifts and blessings, no matter what our circumstance. Build up, rejoice and praise all that God is doing in others. We are free to do this because our identity is firm in Him, even if our world has been rocked to its core. We are unshakable!

Where is your heart? What do your words reveal about where your heart is? When we are grounded in the truth of God, everything will flow from that promise. Our words and actions will bless, celebrate and build up everyone in our lives.

Today's Prayer:

Lord, help me to use my mouth to bless and love others around me each day. Thank you for the amazing opportunities and blessings you have given me in this world. I pray I fully grasp these gifts are from you and that true joy comes from my identity in you alone.

Part Three
LOVE

28
Love Prevails

> *So be strong and courageous! Do not be afraid and do not panic before them. For the LORD your God will personally go ahead of you. He will neither fail you nor abandon you.*
>
> *– Deuteronomy 31:6*

What does it really mean to be well? Really well, deep down in your soul, no matter the circumstance. In an unbearable storm or on top of the highest peak in victory. Overcome by the crashing wave of fear or sailing upon an overflowing river of blessings. I found myself asking that question over and over wondering if I really was well. On the outside, I should be, right? Married for more than two decades with four children, a thriving legal career and a beautiful home, I was far from truly being well with my soul. I was overly busy, constantly worried and fearful. Something needed to change.

I eventually figured it out, but it took time. It's rather simple, really. Ready for it? Just ... love. Love when it's easy, love when it's hard, love when it hurts and when you really want to choose anger or fear. Instead, choose love. Love always wins. It might not always feel good or right, but love prevails ... always. When we choose to take our eyes off of our overbooked schedules, the dirty dishes in the sink or everything else that hasn't gone as planned, we can focus on the blessings all around us. A noticeable shift occurs when homework, clean rooms and completing our daily checklists are replaced with an overwhelming sense of appreciation for what genuinely matters. Love squeezes out stress, fear and worry, until there is no room for anything but gratitude, even in the worst of circumstances. Only then, surrounded by the true realities of life that are thrown at us, can we be truly well.

We have a favorite family video of my son Luke when he was

two years old, running down a grassy hill and carrying a flower when he tripped and tumbled down the hill. At first, he stood up a bit stunned and took inventory that his flower was still intact. He was also oblivious to the video we were filming of him. Instead of crying, he brushed himself off, walked back up the hill, and with the biggest smile on his face, rolled down the hill over and over again. I've watched that video and laughed until I cried too many times to count. It's precious. Such a simple and seemingly silly choice by a two-year-old can teach us a profound lesson.

I've been knocked down quite a bit – most of us have. The choices we make in the best and worst of circumstances reveal where our heart is grounded and help to form who we become. Many times, it's easier to stay down, wallowing in our hurt and pain. To be honest, no one would blame you, but you can get back up. You may not have a smile on your face, but you can take a stand in the midst of fear, pain and anger. Brush yourself off and get up another morning when it hurts so bad, you can't lift your head off the pillow or see through your red and swollen eyes. Put one foot in front of the other and take a step of faith ... then another and another. Get up! Before you know it, you'll be walking again, maybe even running. And if you can't physically walk, do what you can to take a step of faith. In all honesty, you will probably get knocked down again and again. If you keep getting back up, push through that lump in your throat or that unrelenting ache in your heart, you will find love waiting on the other side. Cling to it. Love prevails.

Today's Prayer:
Lord, give me the strength to get up another day even when I feel I can't. When I am paralyzed by fear and I don't have the words, faith or courage to move forward, be all of these things for me. Help me to get up each day and choose love so I can truly say it is well with my soul.

29
Brutally Honest

> *We know what real love is because Jesus gave up his life for us. So we also ought to give up our lives for our brothers and sisters. If someone has enough money to live well and sees a brother or sister in need but shows no compassion—how can God's love be in that person? Dear children, let's not merely say that we love each other; let us show the truth by our actions.*
>
> *– 1 John 3:16-18*

I've been blessed with several amazing women in my life who have provided me with immeasurable love, support and guidance. God gives us unique and beautiful friendships right when we need them, filling needed spaces of grace, perfectly designed just for us. Yet, we all need that one friend who isn't afraid to be honest. You know the kind of friend I'm talking about. For those times when we need brutal honesty. A friend to talk straight with no filter. She's the friend where we don't need to put on an averting mask or veil in an attempt to convince her "everything's okay". No, even if we don't realize it, we desperately need her to push past the facade, pull our mask back and look us straight in the eyes with no agenda other than absolute love.

You may have heard that Peter in the Bible was described as the disciple with the foot-shaped mouth. Enter Julie. I met Julie over 20 years ago. Let's just say she is the Peter in my life. Let me explain. She's the perfect combination of humor, humility, generosity, and brutal yet loving honesty. When everyone else sugarcoats the reality in front of me, Julie calls it how it is. I've cried from gut-wrenching laughter and absolute devastation (usually within the same moment) more times than I can remember with her. She's seen me through some of the darkest moments of my life and held my head up with tears streaming down my face, unable to gather the neck strength to accomplish the otherwise simple task. She's also stood by my side during unforgettable mountaintop moments, where the blessings have been showered upon me. I can go to Julie when I'm overtaken by fear, anger or confusion, seeking her genuine words of wisdom and love. The moments of stunning honesty we've spent together have given me strength to face what lies in front of me, no matter how daunting the road may be.

I remember a specific time when I came to Julie, frustrated with a decision one of my children had made. I rambled on for at least 30 minutes without taking a breath, not allowing her to speak a single word of advice I had eagerly come for. She respectfully listened to my long and dramatic sob story, never interrupting my rant. After I finally paused, I waited for her advice and comforting words of affirmation. For as long as I live, I'll never forget what she said: "Repeat these words Danielle, 'I messed up, but I'm learning and I'm not perfect.'" Huh? Did I hear my wise friend correctly? Did she have the audacity to tell me I hadn't made some of the best parental decisions and I was reaping those choices? Yep, she sure did. I paused for what seemed like a minute, stunned really. Then I burst out laughing until I cried. She was right! I had made some less-than-wise choices as a parent, and I knew it. It was freeing to finally admit it to myself.

In the Bible, Jesus constantly sought out the people no one cared for and loved them exactly where they were. He breathed life into them. He wasn't afraid of spending time with social outcasts and sinners. Instead of walking past them with the same affirming nod the rest of society displayed, Jesus sought them out and genuinely loved them, listened to them and spoke the truth to them. When He did this, people were healed, the blind could see, the lame could walk and the dead were raised to life. The way Jesus lived his life during his time on earth is a perfect reflection of the friend we are called to be. Honest, compassionate and loving.

Julie has helped me reflect on the kind of friend I yearn to be.

Am I the friend who simply nods and affirms when my insides are screaming something different? Am I willing to love deeply enough to be compassionately honest, even if it hurts? Am I totally available, willing to pick up the phone or meet up, even when my daunting schedule tells me otherwise? Let me challenge you to do the same self-reflection I've embraced. Don't miss opportunities to speak the loving truth into others, even if the situation is difficult. Trust your heart and speak honestly with others who are seeking your counsel. Take steps to listen, love and believe in them. This type of genuine friendship is a true gift, creating space for us to believe we can move forward, no matter what the circumstance. This type of friendship can heal a broken heart, open spiritual eyes and inspire others, bringing them back to life.

Today's Prayer:
Lord, help me to be the kind of friend you have created me to be. A friend who humbly loves at all times, breathing life into others by honestly encouraging, loving and inspiring them to be all you created them to be.

30
We're Going to Be Best Friends

> *One who has unreliable friends soon comes to ruin, but there is a friend who sticks closer than a brother.*
> *– Proverbs 18:24*

Craig came home one day and informed me I needed to start dropping the kids off at school. Based upon my work schedule, he had been driving the kids to school for quite some time. When I asked why, he explained one of our daughter's new kindergarten friends had a mother that talked to him every day for at least 10 to 15 minutes. Now, Craig is a nice man, but talking to other moms at the morning drop off simply isn't his style. He's more of a drop and run kind of guy. For months, he talked about this mysterious mom at school that continued to talk his ear off every day. It became a joke in our house when I asked about his new best friend. He begged me to step in and start doing the morning drop off – but I was having too much fun listening to his recap of their conversations each day. He knew what activities her kids were in, how much she loved coffee, how long they had been at the school and so on.

At our daughter's Christmas show later that year, I was approached by an adorable blonde dressed right out of a fashion show. She marched up to me and boldly announced, "We're going to be best friends!" I instantly knew it was her. I soon found out Amy had about 50 other "best friends", but she was right and we became very close. Anyone who meets Amy knows exactly what I'm talking about. She lights up every room she walks into and is a connector of people. Up until that point, I had pretty much kept to myself and didn't socialize with other women from the school. I had been a parent there for several years and had only met a few women I called my friends. After that day, Amy connected me with so many other women at the school, and ultimately bonded a community of us together. She gives me A LOT of hugs, holds my hand, sits on my lap and talks super close to me ... and I love it! She's been such a breath of fresh air in my life and I'm grateful for my silly, funny and genuine friend.

When we are faced with daunting schedules and the stresses of life, it's easy to keep to ourselves and shut out the rest of the world. But we are on this earth to love, to be loved and to live in community with others. When you feel the urge to walk away from an opportunity to meet someone new, push through the uncomfortableness and take a chance on a new relationship that could bring exciting adventures to your life or even create lifelong memories. You just need to be brave enough to take that leap of faith and trust that God knows what He's doing. There are amazing memories waiting to be made with new friends God wants to bless you with.

Today's Prayer:
Lord, help me to seek out new friendships, embrace opportunities to meet new people and be a friend to others in need, even when my schedule tells me I don't have the time. Thank you for the unexpected friendships you have blessed me with that have inspired me to be a better friend.

31
The Swing Set

> *For you created my inmost being; you knit me together in my mother's womb. I praise you because I am fearfully and wonderfully made; your works are wonderful, I know that full well. My frame was not hidden from you when I was made in the secret place, when I was woven together in the depths of the earth. Your eyes saw my unformed body; all the days ordained for me were written in your book before one of them came to be.*
>
> *– Psalm 139:13-16*

Our oldest son was diagnosed with autism and ADHD at the age of five. He struggled to make friends due to his hyperactive behavior and less developed social skills. We never felt there was anything wrong with him; we truly embraced his unique personality that brought us so much joy. We came to realize some people, and especially other children, didn't fully understand his unique way of communicating and playing, but that was okay. We knew God would protect him and he would eventually make friends. He participated in specialized social skills classes with other children who struggled to make friends, and he learned skills over time.

One day, when he was still little, I saw another mom from his school. She ran up to me explaining she had to tell me something about my son. I braced myself for what I was about to hear, because in the past, I was accosted by parents about his challenging social skills or his hyperactive and aggressive behavior. I didn't know this mom very well at the time, but for as long as I live, I'll never forget what she said, "YOUR SON IS AMAZING!" I was stunned and thought, "He didn't push your child or say something socially inappropriate?" She went on to explain he had come up to her while she was pushing her daughter on the swings. He asked her if her daughter was special. She was taken back by his honest and innocent question. She explained her daughter was indeed special and had been diagnosed with Down syndrome. He announced, "I'm special too, I have autism." He then asked if he could push her daughter on the swing. This mother was so touched by his act of love and honesty, she was brought to tears, and so was I!

It's easy to judge other people when they don't fit the social norm, whatever that is. Yet, most of us have absolutely no clue what they are going through and the difficulties they face every day. Before we make assumptions and judgements, we have to imagine ourselves in their shoes. Adjusting our perspective truly changes everything. Instead of avoiding something or someone we don't understand, educate yourself. Instead of trying to change someone, accept them exactly as they are — made in the image of God. We can learn a lot from our children, I know I have. Be genuine, accept everyone and reach out to be a friend, even to those people who appear different than you. You can change someone's world – by simply pushing a little girl on a swing set.

Today's Prayer:
Lord, I yearn to see the world around me through your eyes of love and compassion. Help me to seek out opportunities to show grace and acceptance to others who come across my path, so they experience your perfect love through me.

32
The Letter

> *Therefore encourage one another and build each other up, just as in fact you are doing.*
>
> *– 1 Thessalonians 5:11*

Recently, my older son came into my bedroom with tears in his eyes, clutching a handwritten letter. As he handed it to me, nothing could have prepared me for what I was about to read. Before I read the letter, he explained his little sister had given it to him the previous day. I could tell he was deeply touched by it. Knowing my 12-year-old daughter wrote her 20-year-old brother a letter, put an instant lump in my throat. Gracie is an old soul and I knew I was about to experience something profound. Tears filled my eyes immediately, even before I read it. With each word I took in, the tears welled in my eyes and started to rush down my cheeks. Within two sentences, I had to stop to catch my breath and hug my son. I kept reading. The first part of the letter pointed out the relentless teasing he and his brother had bestowed upon her over the years, consisting of tricking her into drinking soy sauce and coaxing her to jump from the second story of our home onto a bean bag on the first floor. She didn't mention the time they convinced her a bowl of butter was ice cream. You can imagine the look on her face as she swallowed a mouthful of butter! Then, there was the time they encouraged her to break a crayon laying on a table, using her forehead. We actually have that scene on video, for times when we are in need of a good laugh.

Within a few sentences, her letter took a noticeable turn from childhood shenanigans to an endearing sense of love, wise beyond her years. She wrote, "I am so glad to call you my brother. I'm beyond proud of how far you've come in life with the struggles and challenges you have faced. I know I don't say this a lot, and I'm not always the nicest to you, but I love you so much and I'm very grateful to have you in my life."

I've heard it said before, that the most powerful verse in the Bible, is actually the shortest. "Jesus wept." (John 11:35) In this Bible story, Jesus didn't weep after finding out about His dear friend, Lazarus had died. In fact, Jesus was confident he would rise again. He actually wept after seeing Mary, the sister of Lazarus and other friends weeping. Jesus was moved with deep love and compassion for them. As I read Gracie's letter, I wept. I wept because I was deeply touched by the untethered love my little girl showed to her big brother. I wept because I knew I had just witnessed something beautiful our entire family will never forget. I wept because I was proud. I know my son has walked a difficult road, but I realized his sister had been watching the entire time, too. She has been inspired by his journey and has a deep love for him. Even more, she isn't afraid to tell him.

Gracie's letter will leave an imprint on my heart forever, and her words will continue to inspire me to affirm people and speak the words on my heart, instead of letting an opportunity to encourage someone pass me by. More importantly, her words invigorated her brother at exactly the right moment in time, giving him confidence to keep moving forward with the knowledge that he is deeply loved and admired in a world constantly telling him otherwise. I asked my son if I could save the letter for safe keeping. He smiled at me and said, "I'll keep good care of this myself", fully grasping the gift he was holding in his hand.

Today's Prayer:
Lord, thank you for the simple things in life that uplift and encourage us. Help me to live a life of compassion and to inspire those around me. I pray for courage to tell people how precious they are to me and how much I deeply love them. I pray I will not let opportunities to breathe life into others slip away. I will grab hold of these cherished moments and pursue love.

33
Everyday Moments

> Be still, and know that I am God; I will be exalted among the nations, I will be exalted in the earth.
>
> – Psalm 46:10

I vividly remember the day Craig and I were leaving the hospital with our first baby girl more than 24 years ago. We were skipping out of the room with our brand-new car seat, baby bag and sweet Taylor. As we were scampering out, the nurse stopped us. She grabbed my arm and said, "Take in this moment, because before you know it, she will be all grown up." We paused for a moment to politely acknowledge her words of wisdom, but we had absolutely no idea what she was talking about. We blinked and our baby was celebrating her first birthday. Then, suddenly she was graduating from high school. Before we knew it, she was walking across the stage accepting her college diploma. We still talk about the words that wise nurse spoke. We never could have grasped how truly prophetic her advice was.

Birthday parties, graduations, football banquets and dance competitions. These big life events are always eagerly anticipated and documented with hundreds of pictures and video footage just to make sure we don't forget a moment. Yet most times, I've gotten to the end of an amazing event and realized I didn't enjoy it because I was so caught up in the details, forgetting to relax and enjoy the ride. I was missing everything! Yes, these milestones in our lives and the lives of the people we love are amazing and should be celebrated. But what about the everyday moments that are gone in a flash? The simple things. Giving your baby a bath. Cuddling during your 125th viewing of your child's favorite movie. Piling into your bed with your entire family. Taking a walk. Cooking dinner together. Reading a book to your spunky little one, even when you have a thousand emails to check.

Stop. Be present – truly present. Embrace the simple everyday moments you will never get back. These instances are the true and lasting memories we will carry with us for a lifetime. We won't need pictures of most of these moments. They are imprinted on our hearts forever.

Today's Prayer:
Heavenly Father, help me to slow down and appreciate the simple things in life so I don't let them slip by. When I feel the urge to rush through everyday moments that seem mundane, help me to grasp the beauty in even the simplest of experiences.

34
The Crying Bench

> *Two are better than one, because they have a good reward for their toil.*
>
> *– Ecclesiastes 4:9*

I'm a very busy person. Kids, the office, sports, the gym – the list goes on. Sound familiar? Having to stop and deal with a situation that isn't on my perfectly planned out day is usually avoided. In the rush of our crazy schedules, it's easy to pass by life-changing opportunities because we're too busy or don't want to get involved. Many times, though, it's in these unsuspecting moments that we can change the lives of others and forever be changed ourselves.

My oldest daughter, Taylor, started dancing when she was three years old. By the time she was seven, she was dancing on a competitive team. I spent many hours each week at the studio waiting for her to transition between classes, making sure she had her water and appropriate dance shoes. Her studio was in an outdoor mall connected to several other businesses and restaurants. On most days, I would push Taylor's baby brother Luke in his stroller along the sidewalk as we peered into the numerous store windows.

One day, I was strolling by a restaurant next to the studio and couldn't help but notice a woman sitting on a bench sobbing. I recognized her as a mom from the studio, but I had never formally met her and didn't know her name. For a moment, I thought about turning the stroller away and darting down the other aisle of stores, which would surely avoid any contact with her. As I contemplated my escape route, something in me couldn't walk away. Completely out of character for me, I walked up to her and hesitantly asked, "Are you okay?" She looked up from her face buried in her hands with tears streaming down her face. I sat with her for what seemed like hours as we talked and she explained her son had just had an accident. He was okay, but she was scared.

Unbeknownst to the both of us, on that day a beautiful friendship was birthed. She became one of my dearest friends and prayer partner. The Ethel to my Lucy. A few years later, Sheila and her husband Barry stood alongside us at church as our son, their sweet godson Luke, was baptized. We went from strangers to family because we had the faith to be inconvenienced.

I'm so glad I had the courage to stop and listen on that day. I can think of many times when I didn't seize an opportunity and let it slip away. It's easy to come up with excuses or justify our inaction because we don't want to pry or we have enough to worry about ourselves. Maybe we simply feel uncomfortable because we think we don't have the words to offer any help. I've learned it's these inconvenient moments that usually lead to a lifetime of unforgettable memories. The next time you see someone in need, even if they are a stranger, push back the urge to walk away and have the courage to stop and listen. It might just change your life.

Today's Prayer:
Lord, help me to be bold for you and step out of my comfort zone to help others in need. Illuminate opportunities for me to see where I can make a difference in the life of a friend or even

a complete stranger.

35
A Selfless Love

> *Love is patient, love is kind. It does not envy, it does not boast, it is not proud. It does not dishonor others, it is not self-seeking, it is not easily angered, it keeps no record of wrongs. Love does not delight in evil but rejoices with the truth. It always protects, always trusts, always hopes, always perseveres. Love never fails.*
>
> *– 1 Corinthians 13:4-8*

Craig and I met when I was 19 years old. At that time in my life, I had already experienced so much loss. Given my track record with the people I loved, I had pretty much accepted I wasn't going to find true love, and if I did, it wouldn't last. But there was something different about Craig. From the moment we met, I caught a glimpse of his kind and selfless heart. Perhaps that's why I knew he was going to be my husband on that first night. I even went home and told my best friend Steph that I had just met the man I was going to marry. Months later, I found out Craig had called his friend and made the same prediction about us. We were blissfully in love and married two years later.

It's hard to describe the relationship we have. Our marriage hasn't been perfect and we've been through some extremely tough times I didn't know we could overcome. But we did. I often reflect on what makes us work and why we've been able to overcome so much and live with such joy. I've come to realize Craig is a big part of why we have made such a beautiful life together. Of course, he's not perfect, but he's pretty darn close. Without fail, he ALWAYS finds the time to make me feel loved and valued. He walks me to my car each morning when I'm leaving, kisses me and tells me he loves me ... every day. We go on prayer walks and work out together. He leaves me little surprises in my car to make me smile and even laugh (packs of gum, hand sanitizer, floss, you name it) ... evidence he was there. He is the most selfless human being I know.

Craig has taught me a lot and inspired me to be a better wife, mom and friend. I know I have work to do, but I'm getting there. We just celebrated our 26th wedding anniversary this past year. This is what I've learned:

Laugh until you cry.

Let things go.

Hold hands.

Don't take yourself too seriously.

Listen.

Be present.

Forgive.

Love ... always.

Today's Prayer:
Heavenly father, help me to be truly present in my relationships and enjoy the people you have put in my life. Give me the courage to let things go that don't really matter and have a heart of forgiveness. I will be an example of love, trust and joy.

—— *36* ——
Lessons of Love in a Grocery Store

> *Defend the weak and the fatherless; uphold the cause of the poor and the oppressed.*
>
> *– Psalm 82:3*

God orchestrates the most unexpected of activities to rock your world. Several years ago, I had to run into the grocery store to pick up a few things after my son Luke's football game.

He was nine years old at the time. My daughter Gracie was six. The three of us were heading into the store when an older woman walked by, mumbling something under her breath. Her words were clearly directed towards us. I could sense she was bothered by the tone in her voice, and although I couldn't hear exactly what she had said, I heard enough to know she wasn't happy with me. I thought about letting it go and not pursuing it, but then she pointed to Gracie and said (obviously annoyed), "Is she from another country?" Perhaps this is when I should have walked away, but I didn't. I boldly declared, "Yes, my daughter was born in Ethiopia." That's when the woman commanded, "YOU NEED TO TAKE HER BACK TO HER MOTHER, SHE DOESN'T BELONG HERE; WE HAVE ENOUGH PROBLEMS IN OUR OWN COUNTRY." (Now, this is where you need to know a little more about me. Although I'm an attorney and a trained litigator, I don't enjoy confrontation at all, and would never engage a perfect stranger to this type of a debate, especially in a public place surrounded by people I don't know. However, mess with my babies and you've got another story). The fact that she so brazenly expressed her hateful opinion in the presence of my two small children, infuriated me.

I remember looking down at Gracie with tears in my eyes wondering what was going through her innocent mind. The two of them were staring at me, waiting to see what I was going to do. I don't think they fully grasped what was happening. By that point, the woman had started to walk away. Perhaps I should have let it go and continue our errands. Maybe it wasn't my best "mommy" moment, but I pursued her. Holding each of my children's hands, we marched after her. In that moment, I felt such an urge to confront her ignorance and maybe even show her what true love looks like. We engaged in a loud "conversation" that lasted about two minutes, in front of a store full of people who had stopped to see what the commotion was. It was obvious she hadn't expected me to push back and confront her cruel comments. She started back-peddling quite a bit as I exposed her hateful words, and she cowered away. I'll never know if that experience changed her, I hope it did – but I know it changed me. I left the store feeling so blessed and proud to be a mother, a mother to an amazing little girl God hand-selected to be my daughter from across the world.

Later that same day, my family was eating dinner at a restaurant, and as we were leaving, our waitress approached us and told us how beautiful our family was and how inspired she was to adopt. She went on to tell us she too was adopted and had experienced an amazing life. We were in awe of God in that moment.

Jesus tells us to love our enemies. I'm not going to lie, this is difficult for me, especially when I'm confronted by mean and hurtful people. But these people are exactly who we are called to love, no matter how difficult it may be. When we love the unlovable, we squeeze out hate. I probably didn't live out this reality on that day very well, but I learned something. On one unsuspecting day, I saw the best and worst in people. Life doesn't always happen the way we plan out, and we will inevitably be thrust into situations that are uncomfortable. It is these instances that form who we are and can strengthen our faith and love. We are on this earth to love and to spread that love, even when confronted by people we disagree with. I'm grateful God teaches us some of the most life-changing lessons when we least expect it – even in a grocery store!

Today's Prayer:
Heavenly Father, thank you for teaching me some of the best life-lessons when I least expect it. Provide me discernment when confronted with uncomfortable situations to be you in this world, to be love.

37
Get Dirty

> *For everything there is a season, a time for every activity under heaven. A time to be born and a time to die. A time to plant and a time to harvest. A time to kill and a time to heal. A time to tear down and a time to build up. A time to cry and a time to laugh. A time to grieve and a time to dance. A time to scatter stones and a time to gather stones. A time to embrace and a time to turn away. A time to search and a time to quit searching. A time to keep and a time to throw away. A time to tear and a time to mend. A time to be quiet and a time to speak. A time to love and a time to hate. A time for war and a time for peace.*
>
> *– Ecclesiastes 3:1-8*

My husband is a neat-freak. Everything is in order, clean and double-washed. He scrubs the dishes until every speck of dirt is gone before putting them in the dishwasher! If our kids come home from any outdoor activity, you'll hear Craig encourage what he calls a "double washing" as soon as they walk through the door. This means you have to fully wash your hands with water and a lot of soap followed by another round of water and soap. He's even been known to count the amount of soap pumps you need for a thorough cleansing, depending on the activity you've just finished. Additionally, he loves to have everything in order. Don't get me started on his closet. It looks like you just walked into a department store. Everything is perfect in size and color order. Our family has come to love and appreciate his quirky and particular tendencies, but we also have a lot of fun teasing him. Then, there's me. I'm nothing like Craig. While I like things to be neat and clean, I'm more of a quick hand washer and don't need a rubdown with antibacterial wipes or gel whenever I go out in public. Unlike Craig, I usually have a few stacks of things laying around to organize "later", and my pile of clean clothes to put away is a common occurrence.

I believe there is a time for things to be clean, neat and organized. But, many times we are caught up trying to be perfect, never feeling free to just ... be. Take time to let loose and feel the freedom of simply being in the presence of God with no checklist to accomplish. Some days, it's okay if you leave your bed unmade, dirty clothes on the floor or dishes in the sink. Let go of the pressures this world brings upon you and feel free to breathe in His grace and rest in His mercies. Remember to:

> Play in the rain. You can dry off after.
>
> Dance like no one is watching. Even if they are watching, who cares.
>
> Sing at the top of your lungs even if you can't carry a tune. God hears you.
>
> Have pillow fights. You can sleep on them later.
>
> Run barefoot, even if your feet get dirty. A little dirt never hurt anyone.

Make your bed tomorrow, pick up your clothes when you get home and wash the dishes later. Don't be afraid to have fun and get dirty!

Today's Prayer:
Heavenly Father, give me discernment to know when I need to keep a schedule and when to let go so that I can embrace the simple gifts you've lavished upon me without an agenda. Help me to live fearlessly and to enjoy the life you've given me.

38
Progress Not Perfection

> *And we all, who with unveiled faces contemplate the Lord's glory, are being transformed into His image with ever-increasing glory, which comes from the Lord, who is the Spirit.*
> *– 2 Corinthians 3:18*

I'm a work in progress. I laugh and even cringe when I think back on my life and the crazy things I said and did. But there is something inspiring about walking through the fire of difficult times and coming out the other side a bit scorched, but stronger and closer to God. We are not born with all the answers, but we should continue to move forward one day at a time, growing, learning and stepping into our destiny. To be honest, some of us have more roadblocks thrown in front of us than others, but we all have challenges to face throughout our lifetime.

Sometimes, I reflect on my life and sit in awe knowing where my path has led me. Although I've been battered and bruised, I'm stronger, wiser and able to weather any storm that comes my way. It isn't through my own strength, it is only through the power of the Holy Spirit that continues to fill me, guide me and transform my life one day at a time. The process of sanctification takes a lifetime, as we are transformed into the image of God, reflecting His love for the world to see. I've learned to seek God in all things, eventually grasping every area of my life is led by Him. I've grown into a better wife, mother, friend, mentor and leader. Trust me, it didn't happen overnight and I still have plenty of work to do.

Before your feet hit the floor every day, pray God fills you with the Holy Spirit so you see the world as God sees it, through His eyes of perfect love. Every day, pray He will anoint your life and use you to spread His love. Pray for discernment to know what decisions to make. Pray God will do a stunning work of illumination, revealing how you can be His hands and feet in this world. Ask for His blessings upon your life so you can make much of His name. As you seek a relationship with God, He listens, He speaks, He guides, He blesses, He loves and He transforms. Through a beautiful relationship with Him, you will continue to grow closer and grasp His infinite thoughts about you, one day at a time. You are a beautiful work in progress. You are God's masterpiece.

Today's Prayer:
Lord, fill me with your Holy Spirit each and every day. Illuminate opportunities for me to spread your love and have the courage to step out in faith to show that love to others.

──── 39 ────
Make Time

> Moses' arms soon became so tired he could no longer hold them up. So Aaron and Hur found a stone for him to sit on. Then they stood on each side of Moses, holding up his hands. So his hands held steady until sunset.
>
> – Exodus 17:12

My grandmother's picture is in the dictionary under the word "grandmother". Well, at least it should be! She had a profound impact on me as a young teenager. Unlike most 16-year-olds, I lived with my grandparents after my mother had died the previous year. Tackling the rollercoaster of high school, boys, new friendships and sports, all while living with my grandparents, was, in a word, interesting. I didn't know it at the time, but those difficult years produced some of the most precious moments filled with life-changing lessons my grandmother passed on to me.

After high school, I started a tradition with my grandmother where we would go out to lunch every Friday. Throughout my life, my grandmother never had a driver's license. We always suspected she purposely never drove just so we would need to drive her places and spend time with her. Our lunch dates went like clockwork each week. I'd come to pick her up and she'd be waiting for me with her purse in hand, ready for our Friday adventure. She always had the sweetest smile on her face, filled with excitement. We would eat at the same restaurant each time and spent countless hours talking in the car, during lunch or walking around the mall. She told me stories of her life growing up and memories she had of her time with my mom and aunts on Oahu, where my grandfather was stationed in the Navy. We laughed and cried together. Maybe I realized how precious she was because I had lost my mom just a few years before, and I yearned for a mother's love. I rarely ever missed a Friday lunch. I'm so glad I chose to make time on those days when I could have come up with a thousand excuses to not be present. It was more than a quick meal, it was time I knew I'd never get back where I was able to love my grandmother and be loved by her.

Most of us have been given many opportunities to invest in someone or simply be present with them, only to allow the moment to slip away. I know I have. Look for opportunities to spend time with the people in your life. Resist the pull of this world that will always try to convince you to pick up your phone, check your email or focus on your own needs. When you come home from a busy day and your little ones are yearning for attention you feel you have no energy to give, take a deep breath and choose to make time just for them. Read them a story, watch a movie together or just check in on their heart, even when you can't keep your eyes open. Push through the urge to withdraw into your own world and find the time to be present. Make time ...

Make time to invest in others.

Make time even if you have to say "no" to
other opportunities.

Make time today, and don't push it off until tomorrow.

Make time to sit with a friend, even if you don't know what to say.

Make time to love.

Today's Prayer:
Lord, thank you for giving me opportunities to love others and be loved in return. Help me to seek out instances where I can be a blessing to someone and spend time with them, even if I'm inconvenienced. I know investing time in others is food for my soul and the eternal reward is immeasurable.

Part Four
COMMISSIONED

40

Right on Time

> For I know the plans I have for you, declares the LORD, plans to prosper you and not to harm you, plans to give you hope and a future.
>
> – Jeremiah 29:11

Law school was not in my plan. I'm still not sure what prompted me to pull in the parking lot on that day over 20 years ago. I'd driven by the school hundreds of times since it was next door to my undergraduate campus and only miles away from where I grew up. But there I was. As I sat in my car trying to muster up the courage that had escaped me, everything inside of me was screaming, "WHAT ARE YOU DOING?" I eventually got out of my car and headed to the admissions office. My thoughts were racing, unsure of why I was there – but something in me told me to stay. As I reached out to press the elevator button, my hand noticeably shook as I tried to select the correct floor. The elevator door opened revealing a seemingly endless hallway right out of a horror movie. For a moment, I thought about jumping back on the elevator and running to my car, but for some reason, I stayed.

The school was very quiet, and I sat in front of the admissions office for what seemed like an eternity while staring at the daunting door. As I walked into the office, there was not a soul in sight. I quickly grabbed as many pamphlets as possible and ran for the door. But just as I was slipping out, I heard the sweetest voice say, "Danielle?" I thought to myself, "Seriously God?" For a moment, I thought I was losing it. "I don't know anyone here," I thought. I cautiously turned around to find the sweetest woman with a big grin on her face. She looked familiar. I quickly remembered I had met her several months before at a wedding. She smiled and announced, "You're going to law school!" I left the building with a stack of books up to my chin, and before I knew it, I was registered to take the LSAT (Law School Admission Test) and enrolled three months later.

Jeremiah 29:11 is a popular verse in the Bible, used to encourage people that God has a plan for their lives. Yet, most of us skip verse ten, failing to fully grasp the context of verse eleven. The prophet Jeremiah was speaking to the people of Israel who were suffering in exile and in desperate need of hope. They had been bombarded with false prophets who had promised their suffering in Babylon would soon end. But it was Jeremiah who spoke the truth, which in turn made him very unpopular among the people. In verse ten, he prophesied what God had told him: "This is what the Lord says: 'When seventy years are completed for Babylon, I will come to you and fulfill my good promise to bring you back to this place'" (Jeremiah 29:10). Jeremiah was tasked with giving them the news they weren't being rescued from exile for a very long time. This is why we tend to only read the comforting words found in verse eleven about God's plans for our lives. Like Jeremiah prophesied, God's people were eventually rescued from exile. Understanding this context doesn't bother me. In fact, it gives me peace that God's plans are perfect and mine are not. His timing is flawless and I want nothing less.

God's timing and plan doesn't always match our own. It rarely does. We try and stubbornly lay out our life's journey on a perfect timeline, never contemplating that He might have a better path. God graciously scratches our ideas and guides us to our destiny. When an opportunity slips away that you may have worked hard for, be at peace He has something better for you. Knock on the next door, then the next, until your destiny answers. It might take longer than you planned, but keep knocking. Go to God in prayer and seek His will for your life. Ask Him to reveal His promises to you. Trust in Him, His guidance, His plan and even His timing. He will lead you, if you let Him. When you do, you will arrive at your God-given destiny right on time!

Today's Prayer:
Lord, help me to surrender control over my life and trust in you alone. You are the way, the truth and the life. I pray I fully embrace that reality each and every day and release my life wholeheartedly to you, accepting your timing is perfect.

41
The Granola Bar

> *Every man shall give as he is able, according to the blessing of the LORD your God which He has given you.*
>
> *– Deuteronomy 16:17*

After four years as a prosecutor, I transitioned to the area of special education law representing children with disabilities. Since 2003, I've been blessed to be able to work with many amazing children and families throughout my legal career. The thousands of children I have met and worked with have truly changed me.

There is one particular family I will never forget. They had no money to hire an attorney, yet they knew they needed advocacy for their son who was falling apart in school. Diagnosed with autism as a toddler, he was 12 years old, barely speaking and not able to complete simple academic tasks. Coupled with constant self-injurious behaviors causing devasting harm to himself, they needed support. After reading his file, I couldn't wait to sign up the family and advocate for this amazing child. I agreed to take their case on a pro bono basis. Throughout the legal process, the family was always so kind and grateful.

On the day we resolved the case and came to an agreement on a new educational placement for their son, they could hardly contain their joy. We were able to secure an amazing new school for him that specialized in educating children with autism. It was a school where he could thrive. As I walked out to the parking lot to my car with the family, we said our goodbyes, shook hands and hugged. I sensed they weren't able to fully express their gratitude – they kept hugging and thanking me. For the first time, they knew their son would be safe and be able to progress in school.

After we parted ways, a few minutes later as I was putting my briefcase in my trunk, I heard footsteps approaching. I looked up to find my client's father running toward me. He hugged me one last time and presented me with a gift he had retrieved from their car. It was a granola bar. He thanked me over and over again then walked back to his car. I was stunned — holding the granola bar tightly to my chest. As I sat in my car, my eyes filled with tears; I realized I had just been a part of something truly beautiful. "This is why I do what I do," I thought to myself. My clients didn't have much, but they did have love and gratitude. To this day, that granola bar sits on my bookshelf in my office. I glance at it often, and it always brings me back to that day where I learned an amazing lesson about being able to give only what you have – which is more than enough.

There are times when we don't have much to give – emotionally, physically or financially. I've come to realize it doesn't take much to love. Make the call that might inconvenience you, send the text just because, stop by a friend's house who's struggling or cook dinner for your lonely neighbor. It's okay if you don't have much to give according to our world's standards, because sometimes, all it takes is a gesture from the heart – even if it's just a granola bar.

Today's Prayer:
Lord, help me to find opportunities each day to give what I can, even when I feel I have nothing of value to give. Help me to fully grasp that my time, love and attention, may be all that are needed.

42
Take Care of You

> Do you not know that your bodies are temples of the Holy Spirit, who is in you, whom you have received from God? You are not your own; you were bought at a price. Therefore honor God with your bodies.
>
> – 1 Corinthians 6:19-20

I've always been athletic and enjoy working out. After becoming a mom, I found it difficult to balance my schedule and find time for me, but I was still getting to the gym at least a few days per week. However, after I had my third child, getting to the gym was next to impossible. I was spread way too thin with caring for my three children, working and being involved in all of their activities. Before I knew it, it had been a year since I'd done any form of physical fitness. To make matters worse, I wasn't conscious about the food I was putting into my body. Given my crazy schedule, I was eating unhealthy foods on the run and wasn't drinking nearly enough water. I lacked energy, felt unfocused and was overall unhealthy.

I was tired of feeling physically unhealthy and equally discouraged about the choices I was making. So, ten years ago, I made a commitment to treat my body better by pledging myself to a weekly fitness routine. This consisted of working out three days per week and eating better. I did pretty good at first, but before I knew it, I slipped back to my old ways and realized I hadn't worked out for several months. I was so frustrated. At that point, I recommitted myself to get back to the gym regularly, three days per week. I just knew I was going to do it. I reached my goal for an entire nine months and was looking and feeling so much better. But wouldn't you know it, I got busy with the holidays and didn't go to the gym for the last three months of the year. But, as they say, the third time is a charm. The third time, I told myself I was absolutely not going to fail. Whenever I felt I was too tired or busy, I'd take a deep breath and drive to the gym anyway. Not only was I able to meet my goal of three times per week, I was seeing such great results and feeling energized, focused and healthy, so I quickly increased my goal to four times per week. More than a decade later, I'm still meeting my fitness goals and usually get to the gym five days per week. I also set water intake goals each day and am conscious about what I put into my body.

We are all pulled in so many directions. Usually, we put ourselves last on the list when it comes to our health and well-being. Yet, I've found I'm a better wife, mom and businesswoman when I'm healthy, taking care of myself and eating right. We were created body, soul and spirit, yet oftentimes we neglect at least one of these and find ourselves out of balance. Our bodies are a gift from God and we must take care of them. Most of us will make a commitment to eat better and engage in some sort of regular physical fitness routine. But, so many of us get distracted and lose sight of our goals, never getting back on track. The key is, when and if you do get off track, to get right back on! If you fall off again, then get back on again and again and again. If you keep recommitting yourself, you will reach your goals. The key is to not give up, push through the self-doubt and get back up when you fall down. Set small goals, then increase them as you find success. My trick is that I ALWAYS put my gym bag in my car every day so there are no excuses. I swear, it works! When you start feeling and looking better, it will motivate you to be more creative and accomplish goals you never thought possible. Take the first step. You can do it!

Today's Prayer:
Lord, guide me to make positive choices for myself including taking care of my body, eating healthy and being a positive example for my family and friends. When I feel tired and discouraged, help me to push through any doubt so I can reach and surpass the goals I've set.

43
Enjoy the Ride

> The LORD is good to those who depend on Him, to those who search for Him. So it is good to wait quietly for salvation from the LORD. And it is good for people to submit at an early age to the yoke of His discipline.
> – Lamentations 3:25-27

Motherhood has been remarkable. Watching my children transition from each stage in their lives to the next adventure brings with it a rollercoaster of emotions I will always cherish. The ups and downs, twists and turns and moments where you feel you can't catch your breath are all part of the extraordinary ride. We spend so much time focused on every detail of their lives, and before we know it, they're all grown up. It's such an amazing feeling to have children who have entered adulthood, watching them step out into the world, taking risks and chasing dreams.

My daughter recently graduated from college and is living on her own. I've had many conversations with her and her friends about life, future plans and career choices. A common theme I've noticed is a desire to have it all figured out and planned, and if they don't, they are somehow behind everyone else. In their early 20s, they have friends getting married and having babies, which adds pressure to an already burdened generation. Committing to new careers that end up being less than fulfilling can easily lead to frustration. I don't recall feeling the immense pressures our kids are feeling today. Sure, I wanted to go to college, pursue a career and have a family, but I didn't feel the tension to have everything figured out by the time I was 22 years old. Many of our children have received the message they must go to college right out of high school, have their lifetime career mapped out by the time they graduate, fall in love with their soulmate upon their college graduation and get married within a few years.

I started college right out of high school but quickly dropped out after less than a semester. For a few years, I worked as a hostess, an aerobics instructor, a food server, an administrative assistant and even a nail technician. I eventually made my way back and enrolled at the local junior college, older than most incoming freshman. Some would say I did it a bit backwards. I was married at 22 years old and graduated from college a few years later. I didn't even decide to go to law school until I was 25, and graduated when I was nearly 30. Then, after practicing law for 17 years, I enrolled in seminary to pursue a master's degree in Theology. I could rush and get through quickly, but instead, I'm taking my time and enjoying the ride. I'm scheduled to graduate next year, close to my 50th birthday. My sister-in-law, Susie, went back to school in her 40s and earned her marketing degree. Now, she's doing what she loves using her invaluable life experience, passion and joy. She's been such an inspiration to so many women. Her timing was perfect!

There isn't a cookie-cutter perfect plan for you to emulate. Life is fun. Life is messy. Life is unpredictable. With each experience, God is preparing you for the next adventure. Sit back and trust in God's plan. Let go of what you can't control. Don't rush. Learn from your mistakes. If you make a choice and it doesn't work out, that's okay, there will be MANY more opportunities. Try new things and take risks. Seek God's will for your life in ALL you do. Trust me, you will land on your feet and in awe of God's perfect timing. Who knows, maybe your biggest adventure is just around the corner. And, don't forget to take a deep breath and enjoy the ride!

Today's Prayer:
Today I will focus on you, Lord, and what you have for me. I will take time to be thankful for the opportunities you have walked me through and seek your will for my life. I refuse to rush the process and promise to simply trust in your perfect plan.

44
Walking in Power

> But you will receive power when the Holy Spirit comes on you; and you will be my witnesses in Jerusalem, and in all Judea and Samaria, and to the ends of the earth.
>
> – Acts 1:8

I used to love watching the news, but nowadays, after about five minutes, I'm depressed and find myself overcome with sadness. The world around us is filled with so much brokenness and pain. Negativity seems to be everywhere, so we must guard our hearts and not get dragged down into this mindset. Of course, there are times in our lives and the lives of people we love that are difficult, but we cannot live a life defined by our circumstances. Instead of living frustrated and unfulfilled, we can choose to live a life of joy and gratitude. We weren't created to merely get by in life, but we were created to live out an amazing God-appointed mission. We were created with an eternal purpose in mind. The best part is, we aren't alone. God loves us and He is with us. When we invite Jesus into our heart, the Holy Spirit lives inside of us.

Most people don't fully grasp we have the capacity to walk in the full power of God through the Holy Spirit. In fact, most of us don't really know what it means if we're being honest with ourselves. We can live with God inside of us with him speaking, guiding and leading us. I recently heard someone describe how the Holy Spirit is activated within us like a pregnant woman. At first, she knows she has a baby living inside of her, but she can't physically feel the baby. However, as the pregnancy progresses and the baby grows, she becomes more and more aware of the miracle inside of her. She can feel each kick, twist and turn, which impacts the way she sits, stands, eats and sleeps. The Holy Spirit is inside of us from the moment we ask Jesus into our hearts, yet we must learn to tap into the power of the Holy Spirit, which takes time as we grow in our faith.

> *"For who has understood the mind of the Lord, so as to instruct him? But we have the mind of Christ" (1 Corinthians 2:16).*

We can have the mind of Christ and see the world around us as God does, through His eyes of love. We can see what actually can be, as opposed to what is. Instead of seeing the reality of who people are today, we can view others the way God does—in all the glory of their fulfilled potential. Instead of looking at the brokenness around us and accepting the limits of this world, we can believe in the power of God that surpasses any circumstance.

When you feel like you don't have the strength to get up another day, God can be your strength. The key is, you must pursue a deep relationship with the Holy Spirit and nurture it every day to fully walk in His power. Living your life with the Spirit of God activated within you is the most powerful way to live. When you make the decision to live with God's power leading your every step, your life will never be the same. You can be tapped into the most powerful tool in the universe and accomplish only what God can do. Let His Spirit completely overtake you, and you will feel so beyond your capacity ... you will finally be free!

Today's Prayer:
Lord, I commit myself to seeking your Holy Spirit every day in my life, so I can walk in your power and wisdom. Fill me with more of you, Lord, so I can constantly experience your presence overflowing in my life. I want to be you in this hurting world, to spread your love wherever you lead me.

45
It's Worth It

> *But he said to me, "My grace is sufficient for you, for my power is made perfect in weakness." Therefore I will boast all the more gladly about my weaknesses, so that Christ's power may rest on me. That is why, for Christ's sake, I delight in weaknesses, in insults, in hardships, in persecutions, in difficulties. For when I am weak, then I am strong.*
>
> *– 2 Corinthians 12:9-10*

No matter what we walk through, God is with us through it all. He will use every experience to accomplish His call upon our lives. There is nothing that can stop us from becoming what we were born to do. God is NEVER surprised by the difficulties we are confronted with. He is all-powerful, all-knowing and fully able to do whatever He desires to get us where we need to go. Nothing can stop Him! Everything thrown at us will strengthen us, not defeat us. We only see through our human eyes what is directly in front of us, yet God sees us through His eternal eyes, illuminating the complete canvas of our lives. He knows exactly what we need today, in order to live in victory tomorrow. He sees the beauty in our pain, because He already knows who we will be, not who we are today.

There have been many times throughout my life I was convinced I didn't have the strength to get through what I was facing. I've been so broken, with nothing left in me to fight. I felt like I was being chased down by an unrelenting wave that kept sucking me under, where I literally couldn't catch my breath. Death, sickness, fear, broken relationships and betrayal, threatened to drown me. Yet, with each struggle, I began to sense an inner strength brewing within me, pushing me upward. As I surrendered every area of my life to God, I started to experience opportunities and blessings directly tied to what had previously overwhelmed me. My struggles strengthened me and brought me to a place of complete surrender. It was only then, when I was able to hear God speak to me, that I could see His plan for my life and believe I could accomplish it.

Whatever you've been through or are experiencing will not be in vain. Your path may have a lot of weeds, rocks and holes on it, but stay focused on God and He will lead you to the other side. It's difficult to understand you are being strengthened and prepared for your future while living in real pain, but it's worth everything you've been through. You will come out the other side stronger, more focused and able to accomplish the dreams God has placed in your heart. When you feel you can't climb the mountain in front of you, remember God will find a way around it, over it or through it.

It's worth the pain.

It's worth the struggle.

It's worth the wait.

It's worth the difficulty.

It's worth the sickness.

It's worth the discomfort.

It's worth the battle.

Let your story be a sweet melody for your soul. It's worth it!

Today's Prayer:
Lord, I'm thankful for all of the experiences in my life that have prepared me for your perfect plan. Use every trial, tragedy, blessing and gift to strengthen me, so I can become the person you created me to be and accomplish the mission you have placed upon my life to bring glory to your name. Let my past prepare me for my future and change the world for you.

46
Thankful for All of It

> *And let the peace that comes from Christ rule in your hearts. For as members of one body you are called to live in peace. And always be thankful.*
>
> *– Colossians 3:15*

As I'm writing this, Thanksgiving is just a few days away. But, I've learned thankfulness isn't something we should merely embrace one day a year. It's an attitude. It's a choice. An attitude of gratitude and praise for what we've been given changes everything. I love my life, I really do, even though I've had my share of gut-wrenching moments where my world has been shattered on the floor in pieces. Picking myself back up, brushing off, and holding my head high hasn't always been easy during the difficult times. But, through it all, I've been truly blessed beyond my wildest dreams. I've come to realize I take so many of God's common graces for granted. I haven't fully appreciated the beauty and amazing gifts poured out upon me. Many times, the realities of life can drag us down; we lose sight of what is truly important and forget the stunning beauty all around us. Life gets ahold of us and before we know it, years are flying by and we haven't been present to fully appreciate the outpouring of God's love.

Take time to be thankful for the gifts in your life each and every day. No matter what the circumstance, be conscious of the world around you and the blessings that have been given to you. When you stop each day, are truly present with the world around you and take in the beauty of what has been given to you, your perspective changes and you see everything in a new and brighter light. Don't wait for your world to be shaken to its core before you grasp the magnitude of what really matters. Even through difficult times, gratitude generates resiliency. Be present. Be God's light in this hurting world. Be love. Gratitude

is infectious. Today, be thankful for ...
- The sun beaming on your face.
- The air you breathe.
- The magnificence of creation.
- The crisp morning air brushing up against your face.
- Walking barefoot on grass; feeling the sharp blades poking your feet.
- Laughter.
- Taking a walk in the park.
- Reading a book in spite of all the work you need to do.
- The hot sand scratching your feet and in between your toes.
- Snuggling with your children instead of rushing out the door.
- Watching the sunset from your backyard.
- Friends in your life.
- Taking a drive with no destination in mind.
- Eating dinner with someone you love and being truly present.
- Listening to your children tell you about their dreams.
- The ability to smile.
- Love.

Today's Prayer:
Lord, thank you for the blessings you have showered upon me throughout my life. Help me to see beauty and love in the simplest of things throughout my day, so I am aware of the gifts that truly matter in my life.

47
Surrounded by Inspiration

> *Instruct the wise, and they will be even wiser. Teach the righteous, and they will learn even more.*
>
> *– Proverbs 9:9*

I've heard you should surround yourself with people who are smarter than you. Yet, we live in a world which convinces us we don't need anyone else and can accomplish whatever we want on our own. I'm a pretty stubborn, strong and independent woman, but I've learned surrounding myself with other people is key to my joy and success. Different ideas, personalities and perspectives can open our eyes to breakthrough moments, releasing us to the next level. Parenting, business and personal goals are all perfect areas for us to grow in and be inspired by others.

When I first opened my law firm, I loved the idea of being my own boss. However, I quickly realized working as a solo practitioner had its drawbacks. I had come from the District Attorney's office, one of the largest law firms in the county. At any given moment, I had the ability to seek advice from countless other attorneys with more experience than me with unique ideas I hadn't contemplated. I learned invaluable lessons from my co-workers, which I continue to use today. It was a luxury I deeply missed and desired while sitting in my new firm all alone. But, God had other plans.

One day, I received a call from an attorney I had met when I was a deputy district attorney a few years prior. In fact, I had previously been the assigned prosecutor on one of Edwin's cases where he was defending a student who had a disability. Edwin knew I had recently opened my own special education law firm and told me he was the new lead counsel for a non-profit organization, assigned to their special education legal division. This was the beginning of a beautiful friendship.

He asked me to partner as a pro bono attorney for certain cases his organization referred to me, and I gained invaluable experience as a new special education attorney. I am forever grateful to him. A few years later, Edwin called me again. He was interested in opening his own law firm and wanted advice. "Advice from me?" I thought. Didn't he know he was an integral part of launching my firm? I didn't skip a beat. "COME TO MY FIRM!" I insisted. I heard a pause on the other end of the phone as he asked me to repeat what I said. He eventually accepted the offer and nearly 12 years later, we are still business partners, mentors and more importantly, amazing friends. Together, we have encouraged each other to fulfill our God-given destinies, helped our dreams come true and built a thriving business we are both proud of. He has inspired me, mentored me and motivated me to be a better attorney, businesswoman and friend. Given my stubborn personality, it would have been easy for me to walk away from a life-changing opportunity to be blessed with knowledge, encouragement and friendship – I'm so glad I didn't.

Surround yourself with people who inspire you, promote you and motivate you to dream. Don't be afraid to ask for help and seek the opinion of someone with more experience than you. God will bring people into your life just when you need it. Grab hold of the opportunity and allow it to thrust you into your future. Be courageous enough to accept this gift. Be a blessing to others so they can achieve what God has put on their hearts. Breathe life into others. Be an encourager and lift people up to where they are destined to go. Surround yourself with inspiration and you will become an inspiration to others.

Today's Prayer:
Lord, thank you for the gift of friendship and encouragement. I will continue to seek guidance from the people you place in my life to teach, motivate and inspire me. I will seek out opportunities to be a mentor to others.

48
A Walk with God

> *Rejoice always; pray without ceasing;*
> *in everything give thanks;*
> *for this is God's will for you in Christ Jesus.*
>
> *– 1 Thessalonians 5:16-18*

My friend, pastor and mentor, Tammy, has been such an inspiration to me. She has challenged me to continue growing into the woman of influence God has created me to be. She talks about how important our story is and how it has incredible power to change the world around us. So many of us feel our story doesn't have significance, let alone a story that will impact others. Or, perhaps we are ashamed of the decisions we've made and the last thing we want to do is dig up our past and expose it to the world. Over the past few years, Tammy has talked about her prayer walks with God and how they have changed everything in her life. I remember giggling to myself thinking, "I'll never be able to find time to go on a prayer walk each day." I quickly dismissed the idea. Of course, I find time to work out each day on my lunch break at the gym, but I was convinced I didn't have extra time to spend with God. "I'll make sure I make prayer a priority before I go to bed each night," I'd think to myself, justifying my refusal to dive deeper. Priorities!

One day as I was leaving the office at lunchtime, headed to the gym, the Holy Spirit flooded over me and urged me to go to the park and pray. I retorted back to myself, "I'm going to the gym!" At that exact moment, I felt something or someone pull on my backpack and I was literally thrust backward. I was sure I was being attacked by someone in the parking lot, attempting to steal my bag. It took my breath away – my heart was racing! Just then, I looked behind me only to realize my heavy metallic water bottle had fallen out of my bag and onto the ground, which had in turn forced me backward. God reveals Himself and grabs our attention in the most unsuspecting ways. He got my attention. I picked up my water bottle and drove straight to the park.

Since that day, I've been spending time with God at the park nearly every day. I can't tell you how much my life has changed. Previously, I had been more of a situational prayer. I would pray when I needed something from God, instead of diving into a life-changing relationship with Him each day. The most beautiful and intimate conversations with the Holy Spirit occur for me during these intentional moments. He speaks life into me and I've seen doors open I would have never dreamed possible. Fears have been lifted and many opportunities have been revealed, all because I was finally able to hear Him. He's constantly on my mind throughout the day, when I lay my head down to sleep at night and when I wake up in the morning. I'm forever changed.

Faith isn't about religion, it's about a relationship with Jesus. When we spend time with the people we love and invest in them, the relationship grows into something truly magical. Memorizing scripture, attending church and listening to worship music are powerful ways to connect with God, but they can turn into religion if your relationship with Him isn't fostered through prayer. Spending time in prayer with God is an opportunity for Him to change your perspective and reveal why you are on this earth. He will reveal His deepest secrets and desires for you. You will start seeing Him leading you and blessing you beyond what you could ever imagine.

"Now unto him that is able to do exceedingly abundantly above all that we ask or think, according to the power that worketh in us" (Ephesians 3:20).

As we dive into a relationship with our creator, we are transformed by the Holy Spirit into His image one day at a time. Our body, soul and spirit, become aligned with God and we become one with Him. I desperately want you to experience this amazing reality. Will you take a walk with God? I hope so; you will never be the same.

Today's Prayer:
Lord, I seek to spend time with you each and every day. I want to hear from you and grow my relationship with you so I can know your deepest desires for my life and see them fully realized.

49
Whispers of Truth

> The Lord said, "Go out and stand on the mount before the LORD." And behold, the LORD passed by, and a great and strong wind tore the mountains and broke in pieces the rocks before the LORD, but the LORD was not in the wind. And after the wind an earthquake, but the LORD was not in the earthquake. And after the earthquake a fire, but the LORD was not in the fire. And after the fire the sound of a low whisper. And when Elijah heard it, he wrapped his face in his cloak and went out and stood at the entrance of the cave. And behold, there came a voice to him and said, "What are you doing here, Elijah?"
>
> – 1 Kings 19:11-13

If we aren't careful, our minds can play tricks on us and even talk us out of some of the most amazing experiences waiting for us on the other side of fear and worry. Fear can paralyze and stunt the miracles ready to rain down all over us. For many years, I struggled with fear. Fear that something would happen to my children. Fear that someone wouldn't accept me. Fear that we wouldn't have enough money to provide for our children. Fear that if I put my words in print, no one would read them. Although nearly all of the negative thoughts consuming me were baseless and rooted in lies, I continued to get dragged down into the pit of worry. It usually hit me at night after everyone was asleep. I'd lay in bed with crazy thoughts racing through my head, going through all of the "what ifs" I could think of. What if I don't pass the bar? What if I can't beat the cancer? What if something happens to one of my children? What if my business fails? What if we don't qualify to buy the house? The list went on. None of my fears ever came true, yet I let them rob me of countless hours.

One of my favorite stories in the Bible is when the prophet Elijah is running for his life from the murderous Queen Jezebel. While Elijah was hiding in a cave asking God to let him die, he was confronted by a great wind, an earthquake and fire. Elijah wasn't able to hear God, because the chaos swirling all around him made it impossible to hear anything. It wasn't until after the wind was tamed, the earthquake stopped shaking and the fire was quenched, that he could finally hear God's sweet whisper guiding him back to life and giving him the confidence to go on. I've learned God sometimes speaks loudest in the silence. We just need to shift our focus from the chaos of life back to Him. When we do this, we are finally able to hear Him.

We will always have situations in our life that aren't completely within our control. Fear is something we will all be faced with. However, instead of engaging the fear and letting it steal our time as it attempts to pull us into the sea of doubt and worry, we must learn to confront it, call it what it is and turn our focus to the truth. It's difficult to decipher the loud noise of doubt clamoring around in our minds from God's loving whispers of truth. I've often wondered why God's voice is described in the Bible as a whisper. Why would an all-knowing, all-powerful God, who breathed the universe into existence, speak to us in a whisper? Wouldn't the Lord be entitled to yell to get our attention? He's God after all! One explanation I recently heard caught my attention: God whispers because He's so close to us. The lies seem louder because they have to scream to get our attention; God has no need to use tactics like this. The key is being able to understand the difference between the two: Fear is based on lies, while God's word is based on truth. We must learn to tune out the fear and focus on God's voice of truth.

Reading God's word will prepare you for the battle in your mind, giving you the necessary tools to push through negative thinking. Prayer will bring you into the presence of God where anxieties are not welcome. These two weapons are everything you will ever need to be victorious over the clamor of deceit swirling around in your head. What voice are you listening to? Fear will never fully go away, but I've learned to call it what it is and see the lies much more quickly than I used to. As you let the truth found in Scripture sink into your soul, you will start to hear God's voice over the clatter until it drowns out the deception. It takes work and won't happen overnight, but as you dive into God's word and grasp what He says about you, the shouts of lies will be muffled by God's sweet whispers of truth. Remember...

You are loved.

You are a child of the highest King.

You were made in the image of God.

God knew you and had a beautiful plan for your life before you took your first breath.

You are fully equipped for the mission God created you for.

You are anointed.

You can do all things through Christ who gives you strength.

You can accomplish all that you have been called to do.

You have a future filled with hope.

There is a destiny waiting for you when you align your faith with God's will for your life. God isn't in the fire of fear or the wind of worry. He is the calm presence speaking truth in a still, small and all-powerful voice.

Today's Prayer:
Heavenly father, I believe what you say about me in your word, and will focus on that instead of the lies creeping into my mind. I will not let fear steal anymore precious time away from me. When I'm confronted with thoughts of worry and doubt, I will turn to you and focus on what you say about me as your beloved daughter.

50
Too Much & Not Enough

> *Before I shaped you in the womb, I knew all about you. Before you saw the light of day, I had holy plans for you: A prophet to the nations—that's what I had in mind for you.*
>
> *– Jeremiah 1:5*

As a child, when I decided to do something, there was pretty much nothing anyone could do to stop me. This personality trait resulted in getting myself into dangerous predicaments, along with calls from the school principal, notes to my mother from my teachers and consequences at home for my disobedient behavior. Between the ages of three and six, I drove my aunt's car by myself down the street after releasing the emergency brake, fell into our pool on my tricycle without any supervision, busted my lip open on the playground, painfully grabbed a bee hive after climbing a tree, and cut my friend's perfect curls off at school. These are just the highlights, but trust me, there are more. My poor mother!

Somehow, I survived those years of self-discovery as God beautifully wove together my persistent temperament into the woman He created me to be. It took many years and I'm still learning, but He has been faithful to stand by me and protect me, even at my worst. God took my stubbornness and slowly molded it into a perseverance that has carried me through life's most amazing journeys.

Our world tries to convince us to change and be something we are not. We're told we are too tall, too short, too skinny, too fat, too loud, too quiet, not smart enough, not athletic enough, not outgoing enough and not talented enough. However, God created us in light of the world's "too's" and "not enough's" to carry out the mission He created us for. Of course, we should continue to grow and learn, but not with the motivation to become something this world tells us we should be. Our ambitions here on earth should be with our eyes on heaven and consistent with who God says we are. We've got everything we need inside of us with God's power.

There will never be anyone like you. Hold your head high and be confident God didn't make a mistake when He created you and breathed life into you with all of your uniqueness and quirkiness that makes you ... you! Remember, there's never ...

Too much love to spread.

Too much forgiveness to give.

Too many dreams to chase.

Too many people to bless.

Too much of God's power in your life.

If there is not enough of anything, I pray you never have enough of God's grace, love and mercy in your life. I pray you always seek more of Him and His blessings.

> *"When they had crossed over, Elijah said to Elisha, 'Ask what I shall do for you before I am taken from you.' And Elisha said, 'Please, let a double portion of your spirit be upon me'" (2 Kings 2:9).*

When you are filled with all you think God has for you – ask for a double portion. As you step into deeper waters of faith, beyond the shore and into the waves that seem far beyond what you've ever experienced, that's when He will take you deeper, beyond what you've ever imagined. Remember, you are enough just the way you are!

Today's Prayer:
Lord, thank you for creating me in all of my uniqueness for the amazing mission you have planned for my life. Help me to use the gifts and talents you've given me, so I can bless those around me and beyond. I fully grasp I am enough with you by my side and there is never too much of you in my life!

51
Seeking a Breakthrough

> *Do not be anxious about anything, but in every situation, by prayer and petition, with thanksgiving, present your requests to God.*
>
> – Philippians 4:6

Are you seeking a breakthrough in your life? I've talked to many women who feel stuck, lonely and without direction or purpose. Maybe life has become so difficult, they can't get out of bed to do it all over again each day. Sometimes, everywhere we turn, there is a closed door – a child who's gone astray, weight we can't seem to lose, a broken relationship, betrayal of a friend or financial difficulties. Even if your faith is strong and you're seeking God each and every day, stumbling blocks can still be thrown in your path.

Time and time again, I've seen stunning breakthroughs in my life after seemingly impossible trials. The enemy goes after those by whom he is threatened. This deeply impacted me and gave me an overwhelming sense of confidence. I realized I must be on to something if the devil is so threatened by me. If you keep getting knocked down or hit a brick wall everywhere you turn, that's when you need to dig your heels in and push forward even harder. If you feel you are at the end of your rope, you're not; breakthrough can happen if you boldly run after it.

I've been through some incredibly painful circumstances in my life. Yet, it's these struggles that have given me strength and courage to move forward. I've used what I've learned to chase after my dreams and impact the world around me. So often, I sit across the table at my office from teenagers struggling with depression, anger, loss or anxiety. God has so beautifully placed me as an advocate for these hurting children and families because I've been there. I get it more than they will ever know.

I've learned it's in the difficulties and pain where we are strengthened and prepared for our greatest victories. When we feel life has thrown us far more than we can handle, we are ready for a life-changing breakthrough. But, we have to seek it. We have to seek God through prayer so that He will reveal His deepest secrets and desires for us. Where do you need a breakthrough? Your finances, a relationship, a child, dreams that haven't come true or a sickness? Go to God and seek Him first. He will guide you. Chase after Him and seek His blessings every day.

"In the same way, the Spirit helps us in our weakness. We do not know what we ought to pray for, but the Spirit himself intercedes for us through wordless groans" (Romans 8:26).

He listens and hears our prayers before we have the words to utter them. Chase after God and you will experience new beginnings, sudden blessings and realized dreams you never thought possible. A breakthrough is coming!

Today's Prayer:
Heavenly Father, I'm so thankful for the blessings and miracles you are going to rain down upon me. I want to pursue you and hear you speak intimately to me each and every day, so I can have a breakthrough in my life.

52
Revival is Coming

> *For this is what the high and exalted One says—He who lives forever, whose name is holy: "I live in a high and holy place, but also with the one who is contrite and lowly in spirit, to revive the spirit of the lowly and to revive the heart of the contrite."*
>
> *– Isaiah 57:15*

Our world is in need of a revival. True revival is when the kingdom of God breaks into human history, resulting in transformed lives and saved souls — it's when God shows up and moves among His people. We are surrounded by pessimistic attitudes about politics, education, health care and the Church. We find ourselves faced with personal turmoil in our relationships, health, and finances pushing us down into doubt, fear and anger. Before we know it, we can be overtaken by an unrelenting wave of difficulty, unable to move forward. Instead of focusing on the negative messages and circumstance threatening to overwhelm us, we need to turn our focus upward with hope and with an anticipation of triumph. There is danger in complacency and being too quickly satisfied. God has so much more planned for our lives. Of course, we should find satisfaction in our accomplishments, but we must be careful to not take a back seat to the life we were meant to drive toward our destiny.

No matter what stage in life you are in, what circumstance you are facing or what education you have, revival is possible for you. You can be part of a revival our world so desperately needs. Sometimes, we simply need physical and emotional renewal of our bodies and minds to jumpstart our focus in the direction of God's perfect plan. Step past complacency and beyond any negative predictions. Be a catalyst for change and inspiration. Take conscious steps towards the renewing of your body, soul and spirit. Find ways to create moments that are food for your soul, opening you up to new and exciting opportunities.

- Take a trip you've always dreamed of.
- Read a book for pleasure.
- Turn off your social media.
- Attend a conference and find new inspiration.
- Take a cooking class.
- Go to a concert with friends.
- Sneak away for a last-minute weekend adventure.
- Spend time in nature.
- Reflect on your story.

Don't wait for revival, be the start of it with God leading the way. Live it out each and every day, wherever you are – at home, the office, school, church, the grocery store, the park. Everywhere! It's not just on Sundays, but the other six days of the week, too. You don't have to wait until you have it all together, either. The beauty of revival is in the journey itself. Living a life fueled by the love of God fills us with joy and love no matter the circumstance.

> *"But the fruit of the Spirit is love, joy, peace, forbearance, kindness, goodness, faithfulness, gentleness and self-control. Against such things there is no law" (Galatians 5:22-23).*

Be the spark of revival wherever you go! Before you know it, that spark will catch fire and the world will experience revival like we've never seen before.

Today's Prayer:
Lord, today I commit myself to refocusing my life away from the negativity surrounding our world, and instead look to you. I will spend time each day finding joy in the miracles all around me, creating time to renew my body, soul and spirit, so I can be your light of love for others to see. I will seek revival for myself and help to bring revival to our hurting world.

Final Thoughts

I know there are many people from diverse faith backgrounds reading this. You may have picked up this book without faith in God at all. I pray something has been stirred in you. My hope is that you want to know more about the God of the Bible and His son Jesus Christ. The Jesus who saves, who loves and who promises eternal life with Him in heaven. Do you wonder if you are going to heaven? If you have never accepted Jesus as the Lord and savior of your life, I want to give you an opportunity to do that right now. Your life here on earth will never be the same, and you will have the promise of eternity in heaven!

Maybe you have already given your life to Jesus, but through the years, you've gotten off course. Maybe you feel God has let you down because dreams didn't come true, relationships have been lost, or a tragedy tore your heart so bad, that the bleeding has never stopped. You are tired. Tired of coming back to the same worries, fears and anxieties that seem to creep back up over and over again. Tired of looking for love, meaning and purpose in a broken world always coming up short. There is something within you that knows you were created for so much more. Do you need to fully surrender your life to Jesus and be radically transformed by his life-giving love? Do you want God to take control of your life so you can become all you were created to be? Do you want to walk in His power and wisdom and share His love for all the world to see? I pray you will recommit yourself to Jesus, never looking back and always looking up, confident His love is enough. However you came to be in this moment, simply pray:

Lord Jesus, come into my life. I accept you as my Lord and savior. Thank you for dying on the cross for me and forgiving my sins so I can have eternal life. I want to be a reflection of you in everything I do. I want to see the world through your eyes of perfect love. I give you everything I have. I choose to turn from my sinful ways and follow you. Take charge of my life and come into my heart. I leave my past behind and put all my trust in you. In Jesus name, Amen.

About the Author

Danielle Augustin is highly regarded for her inspiration to women to pursue their dreams and fulfill their God-given destiny. Married for over 26 years with four children, she has both heartwarming and painful experiences to share that have beautifully transformed her life. Practicing law for nearly 20 years, first as a deputy district attorney, then as a founding partner at her private special education law firm, her perspective on the world around us is enlightening.

Danielle enjoys speaking at women's events, parent groups, churches and other organizations, sharing her story and encouraging others. She loves teaching, blogging, writing and creating video content about the truth of God's word, equipping women to live a life of faith. Danielle believes in the power of prayer and hopes to inspire others to consistently come into the presence of God, seeking His will for their lives. She is currently in her last year of seminary and will be receiving a Master of Arts in Theology. Danielle has a deep love for the Lord and desires to share the lessons she has learned with other women in order for their lives to be transformed, so that they too can walk in the full power of God and live a life of faith, purpose and joy.

Girlfriend REVIVAL

More Than Just A *Book*

Watch the Girlfriend Revival story unfold in this 4-part docuseries told by Danielle herself at:
GirlfriendRevival.com/the-book

JOIN THE *Community*

Check out Danielle's blog for biblical teachings, compelling stories and inspiration to live a life of faith:
GirlfriendRevival.com/blog

We are on all your favorite social media platforms.

GIRLFRIENDREVIVAL.COM | @GIRLFRIENDREVIVAL

TO BOOK DANIELLE TO SPEAK
at your Event and for Interviews

Contact us at
info@GirlfriendRevival.com
Or visit
GirlfriendRevival.com/book-danielle-to-speak/

SPEAKING TOPICS

- Overcoming Fear, Anxiety & Worry
- Embracing Your Story
- Stepping Into Your Destiny
- Prayer Changes Everything
- Customize any Presentation

TO ORDER BOOKS
for your Group of 25 or more
Contact us at **info@GirlfriendRevival.com**

Scriptural References

Hebrews 12:1-3 (The Message)
Isaiah 40:28-31 (KJV)
2 Timothy 1:7 (ESV)
Philippians 4:12-13 (NIV)
2 Corinthians 4:8-9 (NIV)
Philippians 4:7 (NIV)
Psalm 62:5 (ESV)
2 Corinthians 6:18 (NLT)
2 Timothy 1:8 (ESV)
James 1:12 (NIV)
John 15:13 (NIV)
Isaiah 30:21 (NLT)
Romans 8:28 (ESV)
Matthew 5:6 (NIV)
1 Corinthians 10:13 (NLT)
James 4:13-14 (ESV)
Colossians 3:12 (NIV)
Isaiah 30:18 (ESV)
1 Peter 1:3-5 (NIV)
Acts 16:26 (NIV)
Philippians 2:1-2 (ESV)
Philippians 4:8 (NIV)
1 Corinthians 15:52 (NIV)
Psalm 90:12 (ESV)
Psalm 47:1 (NIV)
James 1:19 (NIV)
Proverbs 3:5-6 (NLT)
Philippians 3:12 (NASB)
Matthew 6:6 (NLT)
Psalm 5:3 (NLT)
James 1:2-3 (NIV)

Romans 8:38-39 (NIV)
Galatians 4:7 (NLT)
Romans 6:6 (NIV)
Luke 6:45 (NLT)
Deuteronomy 31:6 (NLT)
1 John 3:16-18 (NLT)
Proverbs 18:24 (NIV)
Psalm 139:13-16 (NIV)
1 Thessalonians 5:11 (NIV)
John 11:35 (NIV)
Psalm 46:10 (NIV)
Ecclesiastes 4:9 (ESV)
1 Corinthians 13:4-8 (NIV)
Psalm 82:3 (NIV)
Ecclesiastes 3:1-8 (NLT)
2 Corinthians 3:18 (NIV)
Exodus 17:12 (NLT)
Jeremiah 29:10-11 (NIV)
Deuteronomy 16:17 (ESV)
1 Corinthians 6:19-20 (NIV)
Lamentations 3:25-27 (NLT)
Acts 1:8 (NIV)
1 Corinthians 2:16 (ESV)
2 Corinthians 12:9-10 (NIV)
Colossians 3:15 (NLT)
Proverbs 9:9 (NLT)
1 Thessalonians 5:16-18 (NASB)
Ephesians 3:20 (KJV)
1 Kings 19:11-13 (ESV)
Jeremiah 1:5 (The Message)
2 Kings 2:9 (NASB)
Philippians 4:6 (NIV)
Romans 8:26 (AMP)
Isaiah 57:15 (NIV)
Galatians 5:22-23 (NIV)

Notes, Prayers and Dreams
For Revival

Made in the USA
Columbia, SC
22 October 2018